STANDOUT 5

Evidence-Based Learning for Life, College, and Career

FOURTH EDITION

STACI JOHNSON

ROB JENKINS

NATIONAL
GEOGRAPHIC
LEARNING

Australia • Brazil • Canada • Mexico • Singapore • United Kingdom • United States

National Geographic Learning,
a Cengage Company

Stand Out 3: Evidence-based Learning for Life, College, and Career, Fourth Edition
Staci Johnson, Rob Jenkins

Publisher: Sherrise Roehr

Executive Editor: Sarah Kenney

Managing Development Editor: Claudi Mimó

Director of Global Marketing: Ian Martin

Heads of Regional Marketing:

Charlotte Ellis (Europe, Middle East and Africa)

Justin Kaley (Asia and Greater China)

Irina Pereyra (Latin America)

Joy MacFarland (US and Canada)

Senior Content Project Manager: Beth McNally

Media Researcher: Stephanie Eenigenburg

Senior Art Director: Brenda Carmichael

Operations Support: Hayley Chwazik-Gee,
Katie Lee

Manufacturing Buyer: Terrence Isabella

Composition: MPS North America LLC

For permission to use material from this text or product, submit all requests online at **cengage.com/permissions**
Further permissions questions can be emailed to **permissionrequest@cengage.com**

Student's Book
ISBN: 978-0-357-96457-6
Student's Book with the Spark platform
ISBN: 978-0-357-96456-9

National Geographic Learning
200 Pier 4 Boulevard
Boston, MA 02210
USA

Locate your local office at **international.cengage.com/region**

Visit National Geographic Learning online at **ELTNGL.com**
Visit our corporate website at **www.cengage.com**

Printed in China
Print Number: 01 Print Year: 2023

Acknowledgments

Mai Ackerman
Ventura College; Los Angeles Mission College, CA

Raul Adalpe
Tarrant County College, Paradise, TX

Mariam Aintablian
Los Angeles Valley College, Valley Glen, CA

Steven Amos
Norfolk Public Schools/Adult Education Services, VA

Ana Arieli
College of Southern Nevada, Las Vegas, NV

Rachel Baiyor
Literacy Outreach, Glenwood Springs, CO

Gregory Baranoff
Santa Barbara City College, Santa Barbara, CA

Valerie Bare
Chesterfield County Public Schools, VA

Dyani Bartlett
Edmonds College, Lynnwood, WA

Karin Bates
Intercambio Uniting Communities, Boulder, CO

Robin Bitters
Adult Learning Program, Jamaica Plain Community Center, Boston, MA

Emily Bryson
ELT Specialist, Author, Teacher, Teacher Educator, Graphic Facilitator, ESOL Lecturer

Janelle Cardenas
Tarrant County College, TX

Joyce Clement
Chesterfield County Public Schools, VA

Juan Corona
Antelope Valley Adult School, Palmdale, CA

Vasilika Culaku
Goodwill, King County, Seattle, WA

Melinda Dart
Chesterfield County Public Schools, VA

Lourdes Davenport
Tarrant County College, TX

Geisa Dennis
Orange County Public Schools, Orlando, FL

Katie Donoviel
English Skills Learning Center, UT

Reyye Esat Yalcin
Bilingual Education Institute, Houston, TX

Aimee Finley
Dallas College, Dallas, TX

Eleanor Forfang-Brockman
Tarrant County College, Fort Worth, TX

Martha Fredendall
Literacy Outreach, Glenwood Springs, CO

Maria Gutierrez
Miami Sunset Adult Education Center, Miami, FL

Anne Henderson
Goodwill, King County, Seattle, WA

Tracey Higgins
Edmonds College, Lynnwood, WA

Daniel Hopkins
Tarrant County College, TX

Fayne Johnson
Atlantic Technical College, Arthur Ashe Jr. Campus, Fort Lauderdale, FL

Angela Kosmas
City Colleges of Chicago, Chicago, IL

John Kruse
University of Maryland, Arnold, MD

Neskys Liriano
New York Mets, Port Saint Lucie, FL

Maria Manikoth
Evergreen Goodwill Job Training and Education Center, Everett, WA

Sean McCroskey
Goodwill, King County, Seattle, WA

Yvonne McMahon
Houston Community College, Houston, TX

Sarah Moussavi
Chaffey College, Rancho Cucamonga, CA

Xavier Munoz
Literacy Council of Northern Virginia, Falls Church, VA

Luba Nesterova
Bilingual Education Institute, Houston, TX

Melody Nguyen
Tarrant County College, Arlington, TX

Joseph Ntumba
Goodwill, King County, Seattle, WA

Sachiko Oates
Santa Barbara City College, Santa Barbara, CA

Liane Okamitsu
McKinley Community School for Adults, Honolulu, HI

Dana Orozco
Sweetwater Union High School District, Chula Vista, CA

Betty Osako
McKinley School For Adults, HI

Dr. Sergei Paromchik
Adult Education Hillsborough County Public Schools, Tampa, FL

Ileana Perez
Robert Morgan Tech. College, Miami, FL

Carina Raetz
Academy School District 20, Colorado Springs, CO

Tom Randolph
Notre Dame Education Center, Lawrence, MA

Jody Roy
Notre Dame Education Center, Lawrence, MA

Andrew Sansone
Families for Literacy, Saint Peter's University, Jersey City, NJ

Lea Schultz
Lompoc Adult School and Career Center, Lompoc, CA

Jenny Siegfried
Waubonsee Community College, Aurora, IL

Daina Smudrins
Shoreline Community College, Shoreline, WA

Stephanie Sommers
Minneapolis Adult Education, Robbinsdale, MN

Bonnie Taylor
Genesis Center, RI

Yinebeb T. Tessema
Goodwill, King County, Seattle, WA

Dr. Jacqueline Torres
South Dade Senior High, Homestead, FL

Cristina Urena
Atlantic Technical College, Coconut Creek, FL

Marcos Valle
Edmonds College, Lynnwood, WA

Ricardo Vieira Stanton
Bilingual Education Institute, Houston, TX

Lauren Wilson
Shoreline Community College, Shoreline, WA

Pamela Wilson
Palm Beach County Adult and Community Education, FL

From the Authors

ROB JENKINS

STACI JOHNSON

We believe that there's nothing more incredible than the exchange of teaching and learning that goes on in an ESL classroom. And seeing the expression on a student's face when the light goes on reminds us that there's nothing more rewarding than helping a student succeed.

Throughout our careers, we have watched as students rise to challenges and succeed where they were not sure success was possible. Seeing their confidence grow and skills develop brings great joy to both of us and it motivates us to find better ways to reach and support them. We are humbled to think that our contributions to the field over the last 20 years have made a small difference in both students' and teachers' lives. We hope our refinements in ongoing editions will further support their growth and success.

At its core, **Stand Out** has always prioritized robust, relevant content that will deliver student gains in the classroom; while that core mission has not changed, how the program achieves it has certainly evolved in response to a changing educational landscape. The basic principles that have made **Stand Out** successful have not changed. Students are challenged to collaborate and think critically through a well-organized series of scaffolded activities that lead to student application in each lesson. The popular first-of-their-kind lesson plans are still prominent. Features such as project-based learning, video, online practice, multilevel worksheets, and classroom presentation tools continue to support the core series. New to the fourth edition is explicit workplace exploration. A lesson in each unit has been added to explore different fields and careers, potential salaries, skills, and characteristics which workers might have to excel in potential jobs. Also new to the fourth edition, students will be introduced to *Life Online* in tips, activities, and video throughout the series. In addition, **Stand Out** will now be available in different digital formats compatible with different devices. Finally, **Stand Out** introduces a literacy level that will give access through a unique systematic approach to students who struggle to participate. We believe that with these innovations and features the fourth edition will bring success to every student.

STAND OUT MISSION STATEMENT

Our goal is to inspire students through challenging opportunities to be successful in their language learning experience, so they develop confidence and become independent lifelong learners preparing them for work, school, and life.

Scope and Sequence

LESSON 4	LESSON 5	LESSON 6	TEAM PROJECT	READING CHALLENGE
Goal: Identify and prioritize goals **Academic:** Prioritize	**Goal:** Motivate yourself **Grammar:** Future Perfect **Life Online:** Time management tools **Academic:** Compare	**Workforce Goal:** Explore counseling careers **Academic:** Summarize	**Goal:** Research a career cluster **Soft Skill:** Collaboration—Comparing information online	*Protecting the Places We Play* **Academic:** Predict, Categorize
Goal: Maintain good credit **Writing:** Write an outline	**Goal:** Protect against identity theft **Life Online:** Fake websites **Academic:** Summarize	**Workforce Goal:** Explore careers in finance	**Goal:** Research financial assistance information **Soft Skill:** Collaboration—Verify your sources	*Yo Quiero Dinero* **Academic:** Predict

Scope and Sequence

Life Online Video *Page 124*

LESSON 4	LESSON 5	LESSON 6	TEAM PROJECT	READING CHALLENGE
Goal: Compute mileage, gas consumption, and energy used **Academic:** Calculate, Analyze	**Goal:** Follow the rules of the road **Life Online:** Distracted driving	**Workforce Goal:** Explore careers in the automotive industry **Academic:** Categorize **Writing:** Write a paragraph	**Goal:** Create an auto safety handbook **Soft Skill:** Collaboration—Negotiation	*Fully Charged* **Academic:** Predict, Infer
Goal: Insure your home **Academic:** Contrast, Calculate	**Goal:** Prevent theft **Academic:** Predict, Compare, Create **Life Online:** Home security	**Workforce Goal:** Explore careers in planning, design, and construction **Academic:** Predict, Compare	**Goal:** Housing presentation **Soft Skill:** Presentation Skills—Memorize, show, ask	*The Prefab Home: More Sustainable?* **Academic:** Compare
Goal: Identify addictions **Academic:** Analyze, Visualize **Grammar:** Adverb Clauses of Concession	**Goal:** Interpret procedures for first aid **Academic:** Label visuals, Apply concepts	**Workforce Goal:** Explore careers in emergency medical services **Academic:** Analyze	**Goal:** Health presentation **Soft Skill:** Presentation Skills—Make it interesting	*Disappearing Knowledge* **Academic:** Summarize

Scope and Sequence

LESSON 4	LESSON 5	LESSON 6	TEAM PROJECT	READING CHALLENGE
Goal: Return a product **Life Online:** Returning products purchased online **Academic:** Role-Play	**Goal:** Sell a product **Grammar:** Appositives **Writing:** Write an ad **Life Online:** Apps to sell used items	**Workforce Goal:** Explore the role of a customer service representative **Academic:** Interpret graphs	**Goal:** Create an online store **Soft Skill:** Collaboration—Brainstorm ideas	*Eco-Friendly Jeans* **Academic:** Predict
Goal: Identify and resolve problems at work **Academic:** Predict	**Goal:** Report progress **Academic:** Analyze **Grammar:** Noun Clauses as Objects	**Workforce Goal:** Explore careers in information technology	**Goal:** Looking for a job **Soft Skill:** Active listening—Polite disagreements	*The New Workplace* **Academic:** Predict, Summarize
Goal: Interpret information about environmental issues	**Goal:** Communicate your opinion **Academic:** Brainstorm, Analyze **Grammar:** Transitional Expressions	**Workforce Goal:** Explore jobs in community and social service	**Goal:** Give an opinion speech **Soft Skill:** Presentation Skills—Peer feedback	*The American Dream*

NEW AND UPDATED IN *STAND OUT*, FOURTH EDITION

Now in its fourth edition, *Stand Out* is a seven-level, standards-based adult education program with a track record of real-world results. Close alignment to WIOA objectives and College and Career Readiness Standards provides adult students with language and skills for success in the workplace, college, and everyday life.

New Literacy level

**The Literacy level follows an instructional design that meets the needs of lower-level English learners.

Each unit opens with a dynamic image to introduce the theme and engage learners in meaningful conversations from the start.

Unit walkthrough pages from *Stand Out* Level 3.

New '**Life Online**' sections develop digital literacy skills.

An **updated video program** now features two 'Life Online' videos with related practice that aligns with workforce and digital literacy objectives.

Life ONLINE Money In The Bank

Before You Watch

A Look at the photo. What is the woman in the photo doing? What type of things do you think she is doing on her phone? Is it safe for her to be using her phone in the subway?

B Check (✓) what is true for you. Then share your answers with a partner.

☐ 1. I shop online.
☐ 2. I order food online.
☐ 3. I check my bank account balance online.
☐ 4. I deposit checks online.
☐ 5. I pay my bills online.
☐ 6. I send money to my friends or family online.

C You are going to watch a video with advice about how to keep your money and information safe online. What tips do you think the video will give? Share with a partner.

116

While You Watch

D Watch the video. Check (✓) the things Alex talks about doing online.

☐ 1. making friends
☐ 2. shopping for shoes
☐ 3. ordering tacos
☐ 4. playing video games
☐ 5. buying shampoo
☐ 6. signing up for a new credit card
☐ 7. depositing checks
☐ 8. checking a bank account balance
☐ 9. paying bills
☐ 10. getting a debit card
☐ 11. sending money to friends and family
☐ 12. searching for ATMs

E Watch the video again. Complete the tips with the words you hear.

1. Never sign in to your _____ or enter your credit card number while using public wi-fi.
2. Don't give out your personal _____ over email or text.
3. Don't _____ on links in emails or texts if you don't know who sent them.
4. Use different _____ for different websites.
5. Check your _____ and bank account often to make sure there is nothing unusual.

After You Watch

F Read each sentence. Choose *T* if it is true and *F* if it is false.

1. In middle school, Alex wasn't allowed to use the internet.	T	F
2. Alex shops online and uses online banking because it's convenient.	T	F
3. Alex says the internet is very dangerous.	T	F
4. Seeing the lock icon next to a URL can help you decide if a website is safe.	T	F
5. Two-factor authentication can help keep your information safe even if someone has your password.	T	F
6. Alex says he won't shop online or use online banking in the future.	T	F

117

Digital literacy reinforces best practices around privacy, security, finances, and social media.

LESSON 2

The Bank, the Library, and the DMV

GOAL ▶ Interpret charts and compare information

A Discuss the following banking words with your classmates and teacher.

ATM	debit card	minimum deposit	secure banking
average daily balance	minimum daily balance	online banking	unlimited

B Riverview Bank offers three kinds of checking accounts. Interpret the website below.

Riverview BANK	Riverview Total Checking	Riverview Secure Banking	Riverview Premier Plus Checking
With a Riverview bank account, you'll enjoy state-of-the-art online banking and world-class customer service.			
Access to Riverview ATMs	yes	yes	yes
Online Banking, Online Bill Pay, and Mobile Banking	yes	yes	yes
Fees waived at non-Riverview ATMs	no	no	yes
Debit card	yes	yes	yes
Fees waived for checks	no	no paper checks	yes
Monthly service fee	$12 (fee waived if $500 in electronic deposits per month or $1,500 balance)	$4.95	$25 (fee waived if $15,000 total balance)

C Practice asking questions about the bank information above with a partner.

1. Can you do online bill pay with the _____ account?
2. What is the monthly service fee for the _____ account?
3. Do you get a debit card with the _____ account?
4. Can you use non–Riverview ATMs for free with the _____ account?

D **DECIDE** Listen to each person talk about their banking habits. Decide which account above would be best for each one of them.

Life ONLINE Watch the video at the end of the unit to learn about useful bank tips, including two-factor authentication and recognizing scams.

LESSON 2   95

Unit walkthrough pages from *Stand Out* Level 3.

Unit Walkthrough

A new **workforce lesson** in each unit explores the sixteen national career clusters, guiding students to learn about employment opportunities in their own communities.

Unit walkthrough pages from *Stand Out* Level 3.

Team Project

Create a Community Brochure

SOFT SKILL ▶ Active Listening

Imagine that a new family has moved into your neighborhood and you want to tell them all about your community. With your team, create a brochure about your community.

1. Form a team with four or five students. Choose a position for each member of your team.

Position	Job Description	Student Name(s)
Student 1: Leader	Check that everyone speaks English. Check that everyone participates.	
Student 2: Writer	Write information for brochure with help from the team.	
Student 3: Designer	Design brochure layout and add artwork.	
Students 4/5: City Representatives	Help writer and designer with their work.	

2. Make a list of everything you want to include in your brochure, for example: information about the library, banks, and other local services.

3. Create the text for your community brochure.

4. Create a map of your community. Then create artwork for your community brochure.

5. Present your brochure to the class.

Active Listening
Listen carefully
Listen carefully while each team is presenting. How is their presentation different than yours? How is it the same?

Public sculptures, like The Bean in Chicago, are great places for people to meet in towns and cities.

TEAM PROJECT 113

Team projects now highlight transferrable Soft Skills, such as collaboration, active listening, and presentation skills.

The fully updated Reading Challenge will expose students to CASAS STEPS test question types.

Reading Challenge

A PREDICT Look at the company's logo in the photo. What do you think it is a picture of? What types of food and drink do you think they serve at this café?

B Match the vocabulary word to its correct meaning.

_____ 1. brunch   a. money that a person gets if he or she loses his or her job

_____ 2. pandemic   b. evidence that something is true

_____ 3. unemployment   c. a meal that combines breakfast and lunch

_____ 4. proof   d. a disease that happens to people all over the world

C Read the text.

D SEQUENCE Put the events in the correct order.

_____ Carolina collected unemployment.

__1__ Carolina lived in Guatemala City.

_____ Carolina lost her job.

_____ Carolina worked as a housekeeper.

_____ Carolina built her café.

_____ Carolina found a chef and business partner.

_____ Carolina crossed the border with her mother.

_____ Carolina opened Tikal Café.

E On a separate piece of paper, rewrite the sentences in **D** in the correct order, adding in extra details from the text. Sometimes, change the name Carolina to "she" to avoid too much repetition and add transitions like *such as, then, next,* etc.

EXAMPLE: Carolina lived in Guatemala City. In 2008, she came to the US with her mother. Then...

F EXPAND Imagine you are planning a visit to Brooklyn for brunch. What would you order?

62 UNIT 2

Rising to the Challenge

Tikal Café is a brunch and coffee shop located in Brooklyn, New York. If you go to its website, you will see delicious menu items such as Avocado Toast, Winter Porridge, a Walnut Pesto Quesadilla and Coconut Yogurt. You can drink Matcha, Iced Lavender Lattes, or Cold Brew Coffee. But what you won't see on the website is that the café is owned by an immigrant,
5 Carolina Hernandez from Guatemala.

Carolina is from Guatemala City, Guatemala, and came to the US with her mother in 2008. For over 10 years, she worked two to three jobs so she could save up enough money to open her own business. Sometimes, she worked 18-hour days. She used the money from her housekeeping job to survive and pay her bills. And she used the money from her food serving
10 job to save for her dream.

Unfortunately, when the pandemic hit in 2020, she lost all of her jobs. She was able to collect unemployment, but she wasn't happy. Carolina was a hard worker and wanted to work to earn her money, not sit on the couch and watch Netflix. So, she found a business partner, who is now the chef at the café, and picked out a location close to her home. She started with
15 an empty space and eventually built Tikal Café, a neighborhood spot where locals can come to enjoy a cup of coffee and a delicious meal. From housekeeper to restaurant owner—Carolina is living proof of the American Dream.

Carolina Hernandez's hard work made her dream come true.

READING CHALLENGE 63

Unit walkthrough pages from *Stand Out* Level 3.

spark

Bring *Stand Out* to life with the Spark platform — where you can prepare, teach and assess your classes all in one place!

Manage your course and teach great classes with integrated digital teaching and learning tools. Spark brings together everything you need on an all-in-one platform with a single log-in.

Track student and class performance on independent online practice and assessment, including practice for CASAS assessments. The Course Gradebook helps you turn information into insights to make the most of valuable classroom time.

Set up classes and roster students quickly and easily on Spark. Seamless integration options and point-of-use support helps you focus on what matters most: student success.

STUDENT'S
eBOOK

CLASSROOM
PRESENTATION
TOOL

ONLINE
PRACTICE

TEACHER
RESOURCES

ASSESSMENT
SUITE

ADMIN
TOOLS

COURSE
GRADEBOOK

Visit
ELTNGL.com/spark
to learn more

CASAS Competencies Chart

Pre-Unit   Welcome

Lesson 1: Get to know people	0.1.1; 0.1.2; 0.1.4; 0.1.5; 0.2.1
Lesson 2: Talk about personal interests	0.1.2; 0.1.5; 0.2.1
Lesson 3: Write a personal message	0.1.2; 0.1.5; 0.1.8; 0.2.3; 7.7.4

Unit 1   Balancing Your Life

Vocabulary Builder	7.4.9
Lesson 1: Identify learning styles	0.1.2; 0.1.5; 7.4.9
Lesson 2: Identify career paths	0.1.2; 0.1.5; 4.1.9; 6.7.2; 7.5.1
Lesson 3: Balance your life	0.1.2; 0.1.5; 7.5.1
Lesson 4: Identify and prioritize goals	0.1.2; 01.5; 7.1.1; 7.1.2; 7.2.7
Lesson 5: Motivate yourself	0.1.2; 0.1.5; 7.1.1; 7.1.2; 7.1.3
Lesson 6: Explore counseling careers	0.1.2; 0.1.5; 4.1.3; 4.1.6; 4.1.8; 4.1.9; 6.7.2; 7.2.6
Review	0.1.2; 0.1.5; 4.1.6; 4.1.9; 7.1.1; 7.1.2; 7.1.3; 7.4.9; 7.5.1
Research Project	4.1.3; 7.4.4; 7.7.3
Reading Challenge	7.5.1

Unit 2   Personal Finance

Vocabulary Builder	7.1.1
Lesson 1: Organize finances	0.1.2; 0.1.5; 1.5.1; 6.1.1; 6.1.3; 6.1.4; 6.1.5; 7.1.1
Lesson 2: Reduce debt and save money	0.1.2; 0.1.3; 0.1.5; 1.5.2; 7.1.1
Lesson 3: Identify investment strategies	0.1.2; 0.1.5; 1.5.2; 1.8.5
Lesson 4: Maintain good credit	0.1.2; 0.1.3; 0.1.5; 1.8.6
Lesson 5: Protect against identity theft	0.1.2; 0.1.5; 1.6.7
Lesson 6: Explore careers in finance	0.1.2; 0.1.5; 4.1.3; 4.1.6; 4.1.8; 4.1.9; 6.7.4; 7.2.6
Review	0.1.2; 0.1.3; 0.1.5; 1.5.1; 1.5.2; 1.8.5; 1.8.6
Research Project	1.6.2; 1.6.7; 7.4.4; 7.7.3
Reading Challenge	0.1.2; 0.1.5; 4.1.6

Unit 3   Automotive Know-How

Vocabulary Builder	1.9.9
Lesson 1: Purchase a car	0.1.2; 0.1.5; 1.9.5; 7.2.6
Lesson 2: Maintain and repair a car	0.1.2; 0.1.5; 1.9.6; 1.9.9
Lesson 3: Interpret an auto insurance policy	0.1.2; 0.1.5; 1.9.8
Lesson 4: Compute mileage, gas consumption, and energy used	0.1.2; 0.1.5; 1.9.3; 5.7.2; 6.1.4
Lesson 5: Follow the rules of the road	0.1.2; 0.1.5; 1.9.1
Lesson 6: Explore careers in the automotive industry	0.1.2; 0.1.5; 4.1.3; 4.1.6; 4.1.8; 4.1.9
Review	0.1.2; 0.1.5; 1.9.3; 1.9.5; 1.9.6; 1.9.8; 1.9.9
Team Project	0.1.2; 0.1.5; 1.9.1; 1.9.6; 1.9.8; 4.8.1; 4.8.2; 4.8.5; 7.2.6; 7.4.4; 7.7.3
Reading Challenge	0.1.2; 0.1.5; 5.7.1; 5.7.2

Unit 4   Housing

Vocabulary Builder	1.4.8
Lesson 1: Communicate issues by phone	0.1.2; 0.1.5; 1.4.7; 7.2.6
Lesson 2: Interpret rental agreements	0.1.2; 0.1.5; 1.4.3
Lesson 3: Identify tenant and landlord rights	0.1.2; 0.1.5; 1.4.5
Lesson 4: Insure your home	0.1.2; 0.1.5; 1.4.6
Lesson 5: Prevent theft	0.1.2; 0.1.5; 1.4.8; 7.2.6
Lesson 6: Explore careers in planning, design, and construction	0.1.2; 0.1.5; 4.1.3; 4.1.6; 4.1.8; 4.1.9
Review	0.1.2; 0.1.5; 1.4.3; 1.4.5; 1.4.6; 1.4.7; 1.4.8
Team Project	0.1.2; 0.1.5; 1.4.3; 1.4.5; 1.4.6; 1.4.7; 1.4.8; 4.8.1; 4.8.2; 4.8.5; 7.4.4; 7.7.3
Reading Challenge	0.1.2; 0.1.5; 1.4.1

Unit 5   Health

Vocabulary Builder	3.5.8
Lesson 1: Identify practices that promote mental and physical well-being	0.1.2; 0.1.3; 0.1.5; 0.2.1; 3.5.8; 7.5.4
Lesson 2: Ask about medical bills	0.1.2; 0.1.5; 3.2.4
Lesson 3: Interpret health insurance information	0.1.2; 0.1.5; 3.2.3; 6.7.2
Lesson 4: Identify addictions	0.1.2; 0.1.5; 3.4.5; 3.6.3; 7.2.6
Lesson 5: Interpret procedures for first aid	0.1.2; 0.1.3; 0.1.5; 3.4.3
Lesson 6: Explore careers in emergency medical services	0.1.2; 0.1.5; 2.1.2; 2.5.1; 4.1.3; 4.1.6; 4.1.8; 4.1.9; 6.7.2; 7.2.6
Review	0.1.2; 0.1.5; 3.2.3; 3.2.4; 3.4.3; 3.5.8. 3.6.3; 7.5.4
Team Project	0.1.2; 0.1.5; 3.2.3; 3.2.4; 3.4.3; 3.5.8. 3.6.3; 4.8.1; 4.8.2; 4.8.5; 7.4.4; 7.7.3
Reading Challenge	0.1.2; 0.1.5; 5.7.3

Unit 6   Retail

Vocabulary Builder	1.2.2; 1.2.6; 1.3.1; 1.3.3; 1.7.1; 1.7.6
Lesson 1: Do product research	0.1.2; 0.1.5; 1.2.2; 1.5.2; 7.4.4; 7.7.3
Lesson 2: Purchase goods and services by phone and online	0.1.2; 0.1.5; 1.2.6; 1.3.1; 7.4.4; 7.7.3
Lesson 3: Interpret product guarantees and warranties	0.1.2; 0.1.5; 1.7.1
Lesson 4: Return a product	0.1.2; 0.1.5; 1.3.3
Lesson 5: Sell a product	0.1.2; 0.1.5; 1.7.6
Lesson 6: Explore the role of a customer service representative	0.1.2; 0.1.5; 4.1.3; 4.1.6; 4.1.8; 4.1.9; 6.7.2; 6.7.4
Review	0.1.2; 0.1.5; 1.2.2; 1.2.6; 1.3.1; 1.3.3; 1.7.1; 1.7.6
Team Project	0.1.2; 0.1.5; 1.2.6; 1.3.3; 1.3.4; 1.7.1; 1.7.6; 4.8.1; 4.8.2; 4.8.5; 7.2.6
Reading Challenge	0.1.2; 0.1.5; 5.7.1

Unit 7   At Your Service

Vocabulary Builder	4.5.1
Lesson 1: Connect technology	0.1.2; 0.1.5; 4.5.6
Lesson 2: Resolve technology problems	0.1.2; 0.1.5; 4.5.7
Lesson 3: Establish an organizational system	0.1.2; 0.1.5; 4.7.4; 4.7.5; 7.1.4
Lesson 4: Identify and resolve problems at work	0.1.2; 0.1.5; 4.8.6
Lesson 5: Report progress	0.1.2; 0.1.5; 4.6.4
Lesson 6: Explore careers in information technology	0.1.2; 0.1.5; 4.1.3; 4.1.6; 4.1.8; 4.1.9; 6.7.2; 7.2.6
Review	0.1.2; 0.1.5; 4.5.6; 4.5.7; 4.6.4; 4.7.4; 4.7.5; 7.1.4
Team Project	0.1.2; 0.1.5; 4.1.3; 4.1.6; 4.1.8; 4.8.1; 4.8.2; 4.8.5; 4.8.6; 7.2.6; 7.4.4; 7.7.3
Reading Challenge	0.1.2; 0.1.5; 7.2.6

Unit 8   Civic Responsibility

Vocabulary Builder	5.3.2
Lesson 1: Identify requirements for establishing residency and citizenship	0.1.2; 0.1.5; 5.3.6
Lesson 2: Understand your rights	0.1.2; 0.1.5; 5.3.2
Lesson 3: Identify local civic organizations	0.1.2; 0.1.5; 5.6.2
Lesson 4: Interpret information about environmental issues	0.1.2; 0.1.5; 5.7.1
Lesson 5: Communicate your opinion	0.1.2; 0.1.5; 5.1.6; 5.7.1; 7.2.6
Lesson 6: Explore jobs in community and social service	0.1.2; 0.1.5; 4.1.3; 4.1.6; 4.1.8; 4.1.9; 6.7.2; 7.4.4; 7.7.3
Review	0.1.2; 0.1.5; 5.1.6; 5.3.2; 5.3.6; 5.6.2; 5.7.1
Team Project	0.1.2; 0.1.5; 4.8.1; 4.8.2; 4.8.5; 5.1.6
Reading Challenge	7.2.6

For more correlations, including ELPS, CCRS, and EL Civics, visit the Spark platform.

PRE-UNIT

Welcome

UNIT OUTCOMES

▶ Get to know people
▶ Talk about personal interests
▶ Write a personal message

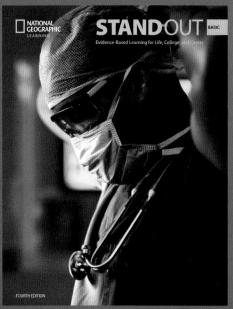

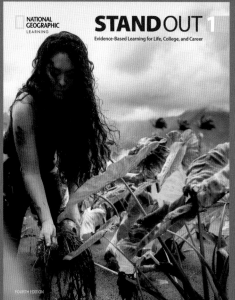

Classroom Community

GOAL ▶ Get to know people

A **COMPARE** Read and listen to the conversation between Sebastian and Rani. Do you know people like them? 🎧

Hi, my name is Sebastian. I'm from El Salvador.

Nice to meet you, Rani. Why are you studying English?

I moved here so I could study at a university and learn how to be a graphic designer.

Nice to meet you, Sebastian. My name is Rani, and I'm from India.

I have been here for over twenty years. I stay home and help take care of my grandchildren while their parents work. I finally decided to improve my English so I can help them with their school work. What about you?

B Introduce yourself to four classmates. Ask them where they are from and why they are studying English.

C Who are the four classmates you met? Complete the chart.

Name	Country	Why are you studying English?

D Read and listen to the conversation between Sebastian, Rani, and Haru. What does Sebastian say to introduce Haru to Rani? 🎧

E Study the expressions below. Any response can be used for an introduction.

Introduction	Response
I'd like to introduce you to _____.	(It's) A pleasure to meet you.
I'd like you to meet _____.	(It's) A pleasure meeting you.
This is (friend's name) _____.	(I'm) Pleased to meet you.
Do you know _____?	(It's) Nice to meet you.
Have you met _____?	(It's) Good to meet you.

F Work with a partner. Introduce them to four people in your class. Make sure you include the person's name, country, and why they are studying English in your introduction.

G Read and listen to Haru as he introduces Armineh to the class. 🎧

Nice to meet you, Armineh.

I'd like you to meet Armineh. She came here with her family from Saudi Arabia four years ago. She has been studying English for three years now and would like to become a registered nurse. She hopes to apply to a nursing program at the end of this semester.

H Choose two people you have met in class today. Write introductions for them below. Use Haru's introduction in **G** as an example.

Name of classmate: _____

Information about classmate: _____

_____

_____

_____

Name of classmate: _____

Information about classmate: _____

_____

_____

_____

I APPLY Choose one of the people from **H** to introduce to the class.

What Are Your Hobbies?

GOAL ▶ Talk about personal interests

A **INFER** Look at the photos. What do you think these people's personal interests are?

1.

2.

3.

_____

_____

_____

_____

_____

_____

B Listen to the conversation between Haru, Rani, and Armineh. Answer the questions below. 🎧

1. What kind of video games does Haru like to play?

_____

2. What are three types of reading Armineh likes to do?

_____

3. What type of photography does Rani like?

_____

4. What doesn't Haru like to do?

_____

5. How late does Armineh stay up reading?

_____

6. What gift did Rani's son give her?

_____

C Share your answers with a partner.

D People have many different types of interests. Look at the three categories of interests. Can you think of some examples for each category?

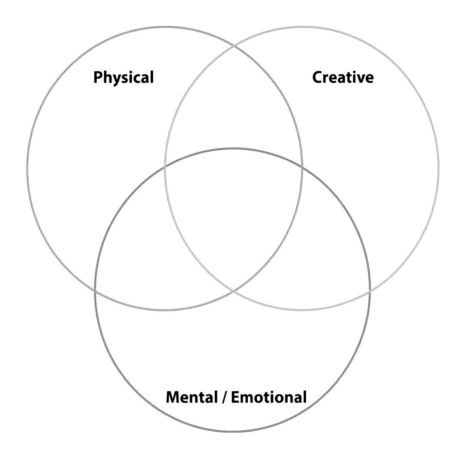

E **CATEGORIZE** Work in a small group. Put each of the activities into the circle in **D** that you think is most appropriate. Some activities may belong in more than one circle.

cook	lift weights	run
do crossword puzzles	paint	swim
do yoga	play soccer	take photos
draw	play video games	watch movies
knit	read	write

F Think about your personal interests. Write them in the appropriate categories.

Physical: _____

Creative: _____

Mental / Emotional: _____

G How would you ask people about their personal interests? Study the phrases.

What do you like to do in your free time?

What are your hobbies?

What are your interests outside of school or work?

H **COMPOSE** Work with a partner. Write a conversation in which you discuss your personal interests.

Student A: _____

Student B: _____

Student A: _____

Student B: _____

Student A: _____

Student B: _____

Student A: _____

Student B: _____

Student A: _____

Student B: _____

Student A: _____

Student B: _____

Student A: _____

Student B: _____

I In a small group, discuss your personal interests. When you have finished, share what you have learned about each other with the rest of the class.

<table>
<tr><td>LESSON
3</td><td># Dear Friend
GOAL ▶ Write a personal message</td></tr>
</table>

A **Read the email that Sebastian wrote to his family.**

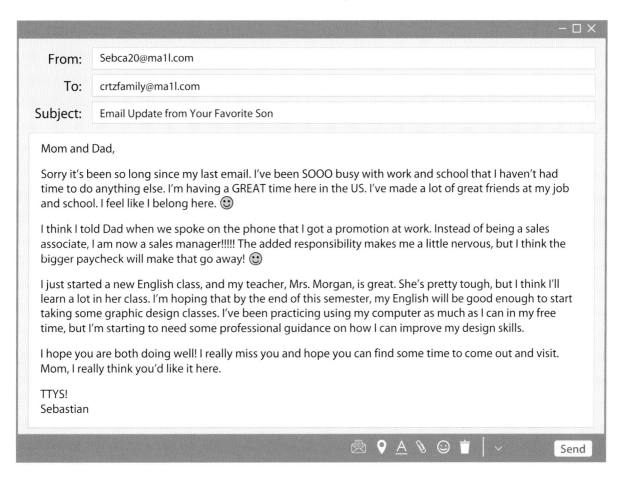

From: Sebca20@ma1l.com

To: crtzfamily@ma1l.com

Subject: Email Update from Your Favorite Son

Mom and Dad,

Sorry it's been so long since my last email. I've been SOOO busy with work and school that I haven't had time to do anything else. I'm having a GREAT time here in the US. I've made a lot of great friends at my job and school. I feel like I belong here. ☺

I think I told Dad when we spoke on the phone that I got a promotion at work. Instead of being a sales associate, I am now a sales manager!!!!! The added responsibility makes me a little nervous, but I think the bigger paycheck will make that go away! ☺

I just started a new English class, and my teacher, Mrs. Morgan, is great. She's pretty tough, but I think I'll learn a lot in her class. I'm hoping that by the end of this semester, my English will be good enough to start taking some graphic design classes. I've been practicing using my computer as much as I can in my free time, but I'm starting to need some professional guidance on how I can improve my design skills.

I hope you are both doing well! I really miss you and hope you can find some time to come out and visit. Mom, I really think you'd like it here.

TTYS!
Sebastian

Send

B **This is a personal email, not a formal email. How can you tell that this email is personal?**

_____

C **INFER What do you think the following expressions mean?**

1. feel like I belong _____

2. pretty tough _____

3. added responsibility _____

4. professional guidance _____

D A personal message is a message that you write to a family member, a friend, or someone you already know. Personal messages usually contain personal information and are written informally. Think of some people that you might write a personal message to. Who are they?

_____

E There are many reasons for writing a personal message. Work in a small group to come up with a short list.

1. _____

2. _____

3. _____

4. _____

F **DETERMINE** Read Sebastian's thank-you note. There are ten mistakes. Find the mistakes and correct them.

Dear Aunt Isabel and Uncle Mauricio
     Thanks you so much for the glasses you sent me for my birtday. They is absolutely beutiful and I cant wait to has a dinner party so I can show them off. It was so thoughtful of you to think of me on my day special. I hope you are both doing well, and I hops to see you soon!
  Kindest regards!

Sebastian

G Rewrite Sebastian's note on a separate piece of paper. Correct the mistakes.

H Mrs. Morgan asked her students to choose someone they had just met in class and send them an email. Read the email that Rani wrote to Armineh.

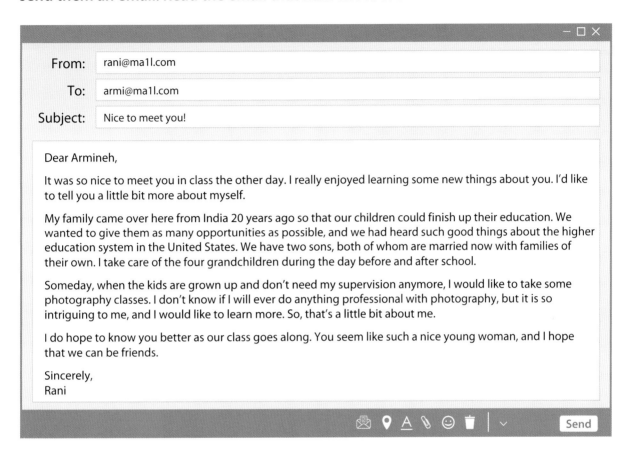

From: rani@ma1l.com

To: armi@ma1l.com

Subject: Nice to meet you!

Dear Armineh,

It was so nice to meet you in class the other day. I really enjoyed learning some new things about you. I'd like to tell you a little bit more about myself.

My family came over here from India 20 years ago so that our children could finish up their education. We wanted to give them as many opportunities as possible, and we had heard such good things about the higher education system in the United States. We have two sons, both of whom are married now with families of their own. I take care of the four grandchildren during the day before and after school.

Someday, when the kids are grown up and don't need my supervision anymore, I would like to take some photography classes. I don't know if I will ever do anything professional with photography, but it is so intriguing to me, and I would like to learn more. So, that's a little bit about me.

I do hope to know you better as our class goes along. You seem like such a nice young woman, and I hope that we can be friends.

Sincerely,
Rani

Send

I **COMPOSE** Choose one of the classmates you recently met and write them a personal message about yourself on a separate piece of paper.

Nowadays, keeping in touch is easier than ever.

1 Balancing Your Life

UNIT OUTCOMES

▶ Identify learning styles
▶ Identify career paths
▶ Balance your life
▶ Identify and prioritize goals
▶ Motivate yourself
▶ Explore counseling careers

Look at the photo and answer the questions.

1. Where do you think this photo was taken?
2. What is the young man in the photo doing? Why?
3. What do you think are this young man's goals for the future?

13

Vocabulary Builder

A Look at the photos and read the information. What can you learn about the students?

Name: Deon
Learning style: visual
Job: graphic designer
Motivation: financial

Name: Ruben
Learning style: visual
Job: photographer
Motivation: joy

Name: Aleesha
Learning style: tactile / kinesthetic
Job: computer programmer
Motivation: fun

Name: Abir
Learning style: auditory
Job: registered nurse
Motivation: time with family

B What do you think each word or phrase means? Write your own thoughts.

1. learning style: _____

2. job: _____

3. motivation: _____

C **INFER** In this unit, you will be working with these groups of words. Make your best guess as to which topic in the box goes with each group. Topics can be used more than once.

career path	learning style	multiple intelligences
goal setting	motivation	

1. _____

    auditory
    tactile / kinesthetic
    visual

2. _____

    earning power
    pursue
    educational attainment

3. _____

    musical / rhythmic
    interpersonal
    intrapersonal
    logical / mathematical

4. _____

    naturalistic
    visual / spatial
    verbal / linguistic
    bodily / kinesthetic

5. _____

    achieve
    balance
    long-term
    motivate
    prioritize
    short-term

6. _____

    be flexible
    evaluate progress
    inspire
    monitor progress
    positive outlook
    support

D Mark every word in **C** that you are familiar with.

E Choose two new words from **C** that you would like to know the meanings of. Use a dictionary and write the word, part of speech, definition, example sentence, and any related words on a separate piece of paper.

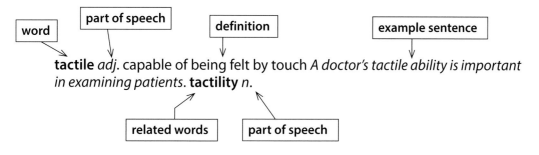

word   part of speech   definition   example sentence

tactile *adj.* capable of being felt by touch *A doctor's tactile ability is important in examining patients.* **tactility** *n.*

related words   part of speech

Learning Styles

GOAL ▶ Identify learning styles

A **EVALUATE** Choose how you learn new skills. Do you . . .

☐ learn through seeing? ☐ learn through listening? ☐ learn through moving, doing, and touching?

B Listen to a lecturer talk about three learning styles and take notes. Write down any key words you hear to describe each learning style. 🎧

Visual	Auditory	Tactile / Kinesthetic
seeing		
body language		
facial expressions		

C Indicate the learning style next to each activity. Write *V* for *Visual,* *A* for *Auditory,* and *T / K* for *Tactile / Kinesthetic.*

1. touching objects _____ 2. looking at a diagram _____

3. watching a video _____ 4. listening to a lecture _____

5. doing a science experiment _____ 6. participating in a discussion _____

7. reading a textbook _____

D **EVALUATE** Choose the learning style you think best describes you.

_____ visual _____ auditory _____ tactile / kinesthetic

E What does *intelligence* mean? Write your ideas on a separate piece of paper. Then look up the definition in a dictionary and write it.

intelligence *n.* _____

F **DETERMINE** Read about multiple intelligences. Underline the main idea in each paragraph.

1　According to psychologist Howard Gardner, there are eight different ways to show intellectual ability. These eight intelligences are described as visual / spatial, verbal / linguistic, logical / mathematical, bodily / kinesthetic, musical / rhythmic, interpersonal, intrapersonal, and naturalistic.

2　Visual / spatial learners tend to think in pictures. They like to look at maps, charts, pictures, and videos. They are good at such things as reading, writing, understanding charts and graphs, building, fixing, and designing.

3　Verbal / linguistic learners have the ability to use language. Unlike visual learners, they think in words. Verbal / linguistic learners are good at listening, speaking, writing, teaching, remembering information, and persuading others.

4　Logical / mathematical learners are good at using reason, logic, and numbers. These learners ask many questions and like experimenting. Logical / mathematical learners are good at problem solving, classifying information, figuring out relationships between abstract concepts, doing complex mathematical calculations, and working with geometric shapes.

5　Bodily / kinesthetic learners express themselves with their bodies through movement. By moving in the space around them, they can process and recall information. These learners are good at dancing, physical sports, acting, using body language, and expressing themselves with their bodies.

6　Musical / rhythmic learners have the ability to appreciate and produce music. These learners can immediately appreciate and evaluate the music they hear. Musical / rhythmic learners are good at singing, playing instruments, writing music, and remembering tunes they hear.

7　Learners with interpersonal intelligence are good at relating to others. They can see things from the point of view of others and they can sense people's feelings. They are good at communicating.

8　Intrapersonal intelligence, not to be confused with interpersonal intelligence, is the ability to be aware of one's own feelings. These learners are good at self-reflecting, and they try to understand their own hopes, dreams, strengths, and weaknesses.

9　Naturalistic intelligence has to do with understanding nature, that is, nurturing and relating information to one's surroundings. Naturalistic learners are sensitive to nature and have the ability to nurture and grow things.

10　In what way do you show intellectual ability? Although maybe you are more dominant in one than another, most people have all eight within them.

G Match each type of intelligence to a main idea.

1. visual / spatial _____   a. nurture

2. verbal / linguistic _____   b. be aware of one's feelings

3. logical / mathematical _____   c. use language

4. bodily / kinesthetic _____   d. think in pictures

5. musical / rhythmic _____   e. appreciate and produce music

6. interpersonal _____   f. express with movement

7. intrapersonal _____   g. relate well to others

8. naturalistic _____   h. use reason, logic, and numbers

H **REFLECT** Which types of intelligence do you think are strongest in you? Write down your top three in order. *1* is the strongest.

1. _____   2. _____   3. _____

I How do you think the terms *learning styles* and *multiple intelligences* are related? Discuss your ideas in a small group.

J Take a class poll on learning styles and multiple intelligences. Which learning styles and types of intelligence are most common among your classmates?

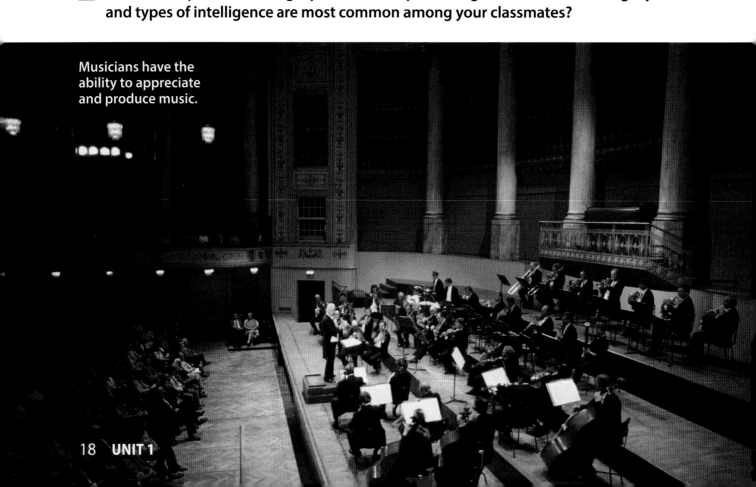

Musicians have the ability to appreciate and produce music.

Career Planning

GOAL ▶ Identify career paths

A What is the difference between a job and a career? Discuss the similarities and differences with a partner. Write your ideas in the table.

Job	Career

B Look up the words *job* and *career* in a dictionary. Write the definitions.

job *n.* _____

career *n.* _____

C Certain careers are associated with different intelligences. Look at the list of careers in the table and write which intelligence fits each category.

bodily / kinesthetic	logical / mathematical	verbal / linguistic
interpersonal	musical / rhythmic	visual / spatial
intrapersonal	naturalistic	

Intelligence	Careers
	architect, engineer, interior designer, mechanic
	journalist, lawyer, politician, teacher, translator, writer
	accountant, computer programmer, doctor, researcher, scientist
	actor, athlete, dancer, firefighter, physical education teacher
	composer, conductor, disc jockey (DJ), musician, singer
	businessperson, counselor, politician, salesperson, social worker
	philosopher, psychologist, researcher, scientist, writer
	conservationist, farmer, gardener, scientist

D Look back at the three types of intelligence you think best describe your way of processing information in Lesson 1. Using this information, choose two careers listed in **C** that you would be good at or interested in.

_____   _____

E In a small group, discuss the two careers you chose in **D** and make notes. What steps do you think you would need to take to pursue one of these careers? Think about the education and training. Make notes of these steps.

F In theory, the more education you have, the more money you can earn. Careers that require more education usually pay more. Look at the graph. Which two things are compared?

_____ and _____

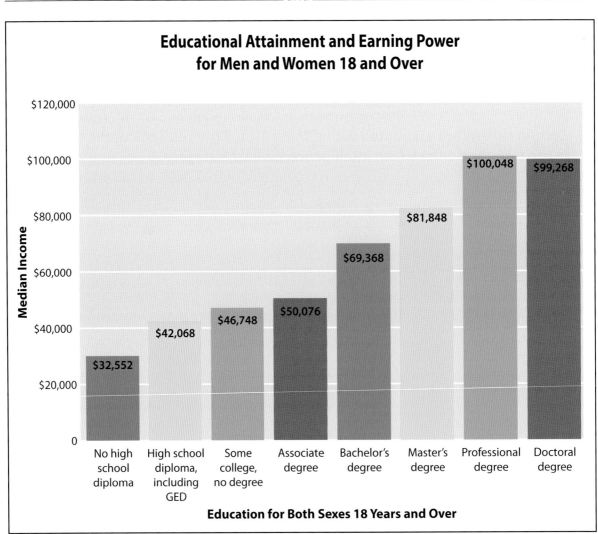

**Educational Attainment and Earning Power
for Men and Women 18 and Over**

Median Income

- No high school diploma: $32,552
- High school diploma, including GED: $42,068
- Some college, no degree: $46,748
- Associate degree: $50,076
- Bachelor's degree: $69,368
- Master's degree: $81,848
- Professional degree: $100,048
- Doctoral degree: $99,268

Education for Both Sexes 18 Years and Over

G With a partner, ask and answer the following questions. Use the information from the graph in **F** to replace the underlined words and make new conversations.

Student A: How much money can I make if I have <u>a Master's degree</u>?

Student B: About <u>$82,000</u>.

Student A: If I want to make <u>over $100,000</u>, what level of education do I need?

Student B: You need <u>a professional degree</u>.

H Listen to the conversation between a school counselor and Sonya. Take notes on the information you hear. 🎧

1. Sonya's intelligences: _____

2. Career she is interested in: _____

3. Education she will need: _____

4. Time it will take to get her degree and credentials: _____

5. What are some other things you learned about Sonya from this conversation? _____

_____

_____

_____

Life
ONLINE

There are many colleges and universities where you can get your degree online. Some programs are through regular schools that have in-person and online classes but there are some universities that are entirely online.

I APPLY Think about a career path you might like to take. Fill in this information.

1. Your intelligences: _____

2. Career you are interested in: _____

3. Education and / or training you will need: _____

4. Time it will take you to follow your career path: _____

Achieving Balance

GOAL ▶ Balance your life

A **Sonya has many roles. Listen and take notes.** 🎧

1. What are Sonya's roles?

_____

_____

_____

Review: *Be*			
Subject	**Past**	**Present**	**Future**
I	was	am	will be
You / We / They	were	are	will be
He / She / It	was	is	will be

2. What was Sonya's role? _____

3. What will Sonya's role be? _____

B **What are your roles? Write at least three statements.**

I am a _____

_____

_____

C **What were your roles? Write at least two statements.**

I was a _____

_____

_____

D **What will your roles be? Write at least two statements.**

I will be a _____

_____

_____

E **COMPARE** Share your responses with a partner. Are they similar or different? How?

F Read what Sonya wrote and answer the questions with a partner. 🎧

Balance in My Life

When I was a little girl, I spent all my time playing with my two brothers. I just enjoyed doing whatever they were doing. Family was always very important to us. But as I grew older, I started working and studying more. It seemed like I was working all day, going to school every night, and studying whenever I had time. I didn't have any balance in my life. Now that I have my diploma, I don't study as much, but I still work a lot. I'm a manager at a restaurant, but I want to become an elementary school teacher. I am also a wife and a mother, and I want to spend more time with my family. I hope to find a job as a teacher where I can work fewer hours but still make enough money to help out. I will really enjoy being home with my family more and having more balance in my life.

1. How was Sonya's life different in the past from how it is now?

2. Is her life balanced right now? Why or why not?

3. What does she want to change in her life?

4. Do you think this change will make her happy? Why or why not?

G Review the chart.

Review: Simple Verb Forms			
Subject	**Past**	**Present**	**Future**	
He / She / It	studied	studies	will study	English every day.
We	put	put	will put	our studies first.
They	worked	work	will work	too many hours.

H Complete each statement about yourself using the verb form and verb in parentheses.

1. (*past*, spend) I _____.

2. (*present*, put) I _____.

3. (*future*, live) I _____.

I Think about balance in your life. What are some things that are important to you? What are your interests? What activities do you do regularly? Make a list.

_____   _____   _____

_____   _____   _____

J Think about how you balanced your life in the past, how you balance it now, and what you want for the future. Answer the questions.

1. What was important to you in the past?

_____

_____

2. What is important to you now?

_____

_____

3. Do you spend enough time on the things that are important to you now? Why?

_____

_____

4. What changes would you like to make for the future?

_____

_____

K Using Sonya's paragraph in **F** as a writing model, write a paragraph on a separate piece of paper about balance in your life—past, present, and future.

L Share your paragraph with a partner and ask for two suggestions about how to make your paragraph better. Write two suggestions for your partner's paragraph.

1. _____

_____

2. _____

_____

Setting Priorities

GOAL ▶ Identify and prioritize goals

A **Read the flyer and answer the questions.**

EVENTS   CONTACT US   ABOUT   SIGN UP

What is your **BIG PICTURE?**

Get what you want out of life!

Attend this goal-setting workshop to learn how to set long- and short-term goals and make your dreams a reality.

Virtual Event ▶

Wednesday, October 7th

5 to 9 p.m.

Click here to register

1. What do you think *big picture* means?

_____

2. What is *goal setting*?

_____

3. Would you attend the workshop? Why?

_____

4. Write three goals you have set for yourself in the past.

   a. _____

   b. _____

   c. _____

5. Did you achieve your goals? Write *yes* or *no* next to each goal.

B **In a small group, discuss your answers to the questions in A.**

C Listen to the lecture on goal setting and take notes about these topics. 🎧

- Goal setting

  _____

  _____

- The first thing you should do

  _____

  _____

- Seven types of goals

  _____

  _____

- Five tips for setting goals

  _____

  _____

D Answer these questions based on the notes you took. Choose the best answer.

1. Which of the following is NOT true about goal setting?

    a. It will improve your self-confidence.

    b. It helps motivate you.

    c. It makes you think about your past.

    d. It helps you choose a direction for your life.

2. What are the seven types of goals?

    a. financial, physical, attitude, pleasure, education, mental, family

    b. physical, career, family, financial, attitude, personal, education

    c. education, career, technical, financial, physical, attitude, pleasure

    d. financial, physical, career, family, education, attitude, pleasure

3. Why is it important to prioritize your goals in a list?

    a. It will be easy to know when you have achieved a goal.

    b. It will help you focus your attention on the most important goals.

    c. It will give them life.

    d. It will improve your self-confidence.

E Sonya attended the goal-setting workshop and created a list of goals that she now keeps on her refrigerator.

I plan to be successful in my personal and professional life. I will be a highly educated elementary school teacher.

SHORT-TERM GOALS	LONG-TERM GOALS
• spend more time with my children	• get my Bachelor's degree and teaching credentials
• exercise to reduce stress	• become an elementary school teacher
• enroll in community college	• get a Master's degree
	• learn how to swim

F Sonya's goals are prioritized (listed in order of importance). Do you think she put her goals in the right order? Discuss your ideas with a partner.

G PRIORITIZE Think about where you would like to be ten years from now. Based on your thoughts, what are your long-term goals? Use these items to help you clarify what your goals should be.

1. Write one goal for each category.

   Education: _____

   Career: _____

   Family: _____

   Financial: _____

   Physical: _____

   Attitude: _____

   Pleasure: _____

2. Number your three most important goals above in order of priority.

   _____

3. What are some short-term goals you can set in order to help you reach the three long-term goals you chose?

   Short-term goals: _____

   _____

4. Prioritize your short-term goals. Write them in order. _____

   _____

Motivation

GOAL ▶ Motivate yourself

A What does *motivation* mean?

motivation *n.* (your own definition or one from a dictionary): _____

_____

B How can you motivate yourself to reach your goals? Work in a small group and make a list.

_____

_____

_____

_____

C Listen to Mrs. Morgan's students talk about motivating themselves. Take notes about what each person says. 🎧

Deon: _____

_____

_____

Sonya: _____

_____

_____

Ruben: _____

_____

_____

Aleesha: _____

_____

_____

Abir: _____

_____

_____

Mario: _____

_____

_____

D What idea for getting motivated does each person in **C** have? Share what you recall with a partner.

E Read the list of steps you can take to motivate yourself toward pursuing a goal. Mark the steps you already do and the steps you would like to do.

I already do	I would like to do	Steps to motivate yourself toward pursuing a goal
		1. Write down your goals and put them in a place you will see them every day.
		2. Put a reminder on your phone that pops up every day to remind you of your goal.
		3. Tell yourself that you can do it.
		4. Keep a positive attitude.
		5. Be enthusiastic about your goals.
		6. When you slow down or don't have the energy to do anything, take small steps and continue moving forward. Don't stop.
		7. Evaluate your progress. Make a chart or do something to monitor progress.
		8. Don't be too fixed on one approach. Be flexible and make changes when needed.
		9. Read inspiring books.
		10. Take some time to refresh yourself.
		11. Exercise more to help your attitude. The better your health, the more positive your outlook.
		12. After you are motivated, motivate others.

F COMPARE Share your list with a partner. Are there any steps that both of you would like to take? What are your differences?

G Study the chart with your teacher.

Future Perfect				
Subject	*will have*	Past Participle		Future Event—Time Expression
I	will have	become	a teacher	**by** the time my kids are in school.
He	will have	been	a graphic designer (for five years)	**when** he turns 35.
They	will have	found	a job	**by** next year.

We use the future perfect to talk about an activity that will be completed before another time or event in the future. |present ✕ future to be completed (perfect) ✕ future event with time expression

Note: The order of events is not important. If the future event with the time expression comes first, use a comma.

Example: *By the time my kids are in school, I will have become a teacher.*

H Mrs. Morgan's students wrote goal statements. Complete each statement with the correct form of the future perfect.

1. By the time I graduate from high school, I _____ (do) 500 hours of community service.

2. I _____ (buy) a new house when I retire.

3. When I turn 60, I _____ (travel) to over 20 states.

4. We _____ (put) three kids through college by 2030.

5. I _____ (become) a successful business owner by the time I turn 40.

6. By the time I finish getting my degree, I _____ (apply) to three different graduate programs.

I Write three goal statements for yourself on a separate piece of paper. Use the future perfect.

J Now that you have written your goals, what are you going to do to keep yourself motivated to achieve these specific goals? Write three ideas.

_____

_____

_____

_____

_____

LESSON 6

Explore the Workforce

GOAL ▶ Explore counseling careers

A How would you define *counselor*? Write your idea. Then look the word up and write the dictionary definition.

Counselor *n.*

My definition: _____

Dictionary definition: _____

B There are over 50 different types of counselors. Some of them are on this list. Decide which counselor would be best for each person.

Addiction Counselor	High School Counselor
Alcohol and Drug Abuse Counselor	Juvenile Justice Counselor
Anger Management Counselor	Marriage Counselor
Career Development Counselor	Mental Health Counselor
Domestic Violence Counselor	Nutritional Counselor
Eating Disorder Counselor	Vocational Counselor
Elementary School Counselor	Rehabilitation Counselor
Family Counselor	Sports Counselor
Grief Counselor	Veteran's Counselor

1. My father passed away last month. I'm having trouble dealing with his death. _grief counselor_

2. Abdul is hoping to become a lawyer. He needs help with how to make that happen in the US.
   _____

3. Sometimes, I get so mad, I throw things and punch holes in my apartment wall.
   _____

4. Sofia and Dmitri have been yelling at each other more and more in front of their kids.
   _____

5. My doctor said my cholesterol is high and I need to start eating better.
   _____

6. Jaynie's teenage son needs to figure out his class schedule for next year.
   _____

7. Her father has never been the same since he returned from fighting in the military.

_____

8. Khadija is sad and never wants to leave the house. _____

9. My uncle spends all his money in casinos. I'm worried he is going to lose everything.

_____

10. Jamal is a college football player who is having confidence issues when he gets on the field.

_____

C Recently, there has been a rise in the need for counselors due to depression, physical abuse, and mental health disorders. This graph shows the projected growth in counseling jobs over 10 years. Do the numbers surprise you? Why or why not?

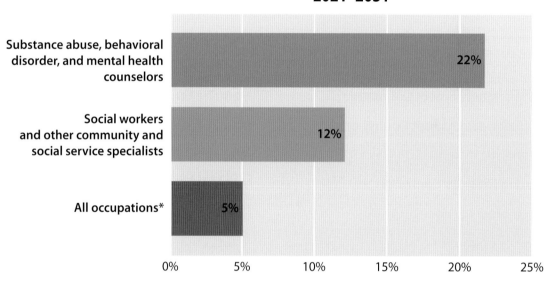

Projected Change in Employment 2021–2031

* *All occupations* refers to all other occupations in the United States. SOURCE: www.bls.gov

D Listen and fill in the missing words. 🎧

Jobs for substance abuse, behavioral disorder, and mental health counselors are projected to increase (1) _____ percent from 2021 to (2) _____, which is much faster than the average for all occupations. About (3) _____ job openings on average for substance abuse, behavioral disorder, and (4) _____ counselors are projected each year over the next ten years. Many of those openings will be a result of workers transferring to different occupations or (5) _____ for various reasons, such as retirement.

Employment is (6) _____ for substance abuse, behavioral disorder, and mental health counselors since more and more people are looking for help with

(7) _____ and mental health issues. The (8) _____ for these counselors is also expected to increase as (9) _____ and counseling services instead of jail time for people with addictions or mental health concerns. In addition, there will be a continued need for mental health and substance abuse counseling for (10) _____.

E There is one type of counselor that has not been listed because the Bureau of Labor Statistics does not collect data on it yet. This counselor is a life coach. What do you think a life coach does? Brainstorm some ideas.

A life coach:

1. _____

2. _____

3. _____

4. _____

F **SUMMARIZE** Read. Then explain to a partner (without reading) how to become a life coach.

How to Become a Life Coach

1. Complete a training program from an accredited industry association. This can take 18–24 months and cost between $2,500 and $12,000.

2. Get certified. Certification requires 500 hours of coaching experience (450 paid), as well as at least 25 clients.

3. Take and pass a test.

G Imagine you hired a life coach. Give each item a percentage based on how much help you need in that area (some may be 0%). The total should equal 100%.

_____ Academic issues   _____ Physical health

_____ Aging   _____ Romantic relationships

_____ Business

_____ Career transition   _____ Spirituality
and job search
                               _____ Work-life balance

H Create a pie chart with the percentages and the circle in **G**.

Review

A Indicate the learning style next to each activity. Write *V* for *Visual, A* for *Auditory,* and *T / K* for *Tactile / Kinesthetic.*

1. analyzing a graph _____

2. reading a journal article _____

3. listening to a discussion _____

4. touching objects _____

5. listening to a podcast _____

6. watching the news online _____

7. participating in a dance _____

B Complete each statement with a phrase from the box.

appreciates music	relates well to surroundings
expresses oneself with movement	thinks in pictures
is aware of one's own feelings	uses language
relates well to others	uses reason, logic, and numbers

1. A naturalistic person _____.

2. Someone with interpersonal intelligence _____.

3. A person who is kinesthetic _____.

4. A logical / mathematical person _____.

5. A person with visual intelligence _____.

6. Someone with intrapersonal intelligence _____.

7. A musical / rhythmic person _____.

8. A verbal / linguistic person _____.

C Ask a classmate how they relate to this information. Write their answers.

1. Types of intelligence: _____

2. Career interests: _____

3. What is important to you now? _____

4. What changes would you like to make for your future? _____

_____

Learner Log	I can identify learning styles.	I can identify career paths.
	☐ Yes ☐ No ☐ Maybe	☐ Yes ☐ No ☐ Maybe

D Write a paragraph about your partner on a separate piece of paper using the information from C.

E Remember what you learned about goal setting. Without looking back, write four tips for setting goals.

1. _____

2. _____

3. _____

4. _____

F Walk around the classroom and ask your classmates for suggestions on how to motivate yourself. Write five ideas.

1. _____

2. _____

3. _____

4. _____

5. _____

G Choose a verb from the box and complete each goal statement with the correct form of the future perfect.

apply	compete	work
buy and sell	program	

1. By the time I graduate from technical school, I _____ over 20 computers.

2. She _____ at least ten properties when she retires.

3. When he retires, he _____ for 35 years.

4. They _____ in their first triathlon by the year 2030.

5. By the time I get my Master's degree, I _____ for 40 jobs at companies all over the country.

Vocabulary Review

Use these words and phrases to help you complete all the exercises on this page. Some words may be used more than once.

achieve	evaluate	positive outlook
balance	inspire	prioritize
be flexible	long-term	pursue
earning power	monitor	short-term
educational attainment	motivate	support

A **Complete each sentence with the best verb. Some sentences can have more than one answer. Then work with a partner and use the six questions for a discussion.**

1. If you _____ your goals, you can focus on the most important ones first.

2. Have you ever created a chart to _____ your progress?

3. What career do you think you might _____?

4. How do you _____ yourself?

5. What goals have you wanted to _____ in the past?

6. Have you found family and friends who _____ you?

B **Write sentences about goal setting with these terms from the vocabulary box.**

1. balance: _____

2. be flexible: _____

3. positive outlook: _____

4. achieve: _____

C **Complete each sentence.**

1. To improve your earning power, you should _____
   _____.

2. If you want to achieve your goals, you must _____
   _____.

3. In order to best reach your long-term goals, you have to _____
   _____.

Research Project

Research a Career Cluster

SOFT SKILL ▶ Collaboration

A One of the fastest ways to research something is to search the internet. For example, you might want to know how much money you can make in a certain career. What are some key words you could use to search for this information?

_____

B Conduct an online search to find out this information for the career path that you chose in I in Lesson 2.

Career title: _____

Training needed: _____

Education needed: _____

Possible earnings: _____

C The Bureau of Labor Statistics is a US government organization that collects data about jobs and careers. These career clusters are from the *Occupational Outlook Handbook*. Underline the cluster you think would have information about your career.

Agriculture, Foods, and Natural Resources

Architecture and Construction

Arts, Audio/Video Technology, and Communications

Business Management and Administration

Education and Training

Finance

Government and Public Administration

Health Science

Hospitality and Tourism

Human Services

Information Technology

Law, Public Safety, Corrections, and Security

Manufacturing

Marketing

Science, Technology, Engineering, and Mathematics

Transportation Distribution and Logistics

D Find the *Occupational Outlook Handbook* online at bls.gov. Search for information about your chosen career.

COLLABORATION

Comparing information online

When doing research online, it is important to look for data from more than one site. Compare the information you found in **B** with what you found in **D**. Is it the same? Is one site more reputable than another?

RESEARCH PROJECT 37

Reading Challenge

A **PREDICT** Trip Jennings is a filmmaker and a professional kayaker. How do you think these two things could be related?

_____

_____

B Match each word to the best definition.

_____ 1. conservationist

_____ 2. destruction

_____ 3. document

_____ 4. produce

_____ 5. social justice

a. _v._ to bring something into existence

b. _v._ to support with factual evidence, written or visual

c. _n._ a person who tries to prevent waste or loss of natural resources

d. _n._ fair treatment of all people

e. _n._ reduction to a useless form; ruin

C Read _Protecting the Places We Play_. Think about Trip's multiple intelligences.

D **CATEGORIZE** Find examples in the reading of Trip's multiple intelligences. Write an example and the line number where you found it.

Intelligence	Example	Line
visual / spatial	watched videos	2
bodily / kinesthetic		
interpersonal		
naturalistic		

E Answer the questions on a separate piece of paper.

1. How does Trip work to "protect the wild lands, wild animals, and the places we play"?

2. Why do you think Trip decided to start making films about kayaking?

3. What caused his filmmaking purpose to change?

4. Think about Trip's normal day. How is it different from yours? Is it similar to yours in any way? How do you think he finds balance?

Protecting the Places We Play

Trip Jennings is a filmmaker who loves to kayak. Or should that be a professional kayaker who loves to make films? Watching kayaking videos as a child, he decided that he wanted to be the one behind the camera. For years, he kayaked and produced whitewater* kayaking videos, documenting some of the most beautiful places in the world. But to get to those amazing places,
5 he had to travel through places where the environment had been destroyed. This caused him to rethink the purpose of his filmmaking.

In addition to being an award-winning filmmaker, kayaker, and adventurer, Trip is a conservationist. He spends his time working to protect rivers around the world. He also documents fossil fuel extraction, mining, and energy export in North America. To help get his
10 message out, he runs a video production company called Balance Media. The company focuses on telling stories through videography for environmental and social justice organizations. He is also on the advisory board of Adventurers and Scientists for Conservation (ASC), which brings adventurers and scientists together to share data collected from around the world.

With everything that Trip has going on, it is often hard to stay balanced. When asked what
15 a normal day is like for him, this is what he said: "I spend a fair amount of my time wishing for normal days, trying to find balance. I'm out and about for around half the year, traveling, filming, and working on conservation projects. In 2011, that led me to the Democratic Republic of the Congo, Canada three times, Mexico, and a number of trips within the US. The rest of the year I spend editing, fundraising, and planning—all of the office work that makes the fieldwork
20 possible and useful. So, half the year I'm waking up at sunrise in the wilderness, getting dirty, carrying cameras into the backcountry, and documenting beauty and destruction. The other half, I'm waking up and walking to my Portland office to click and drag most of the day."

---

whitewater: fast-moving and shallow stretches of water

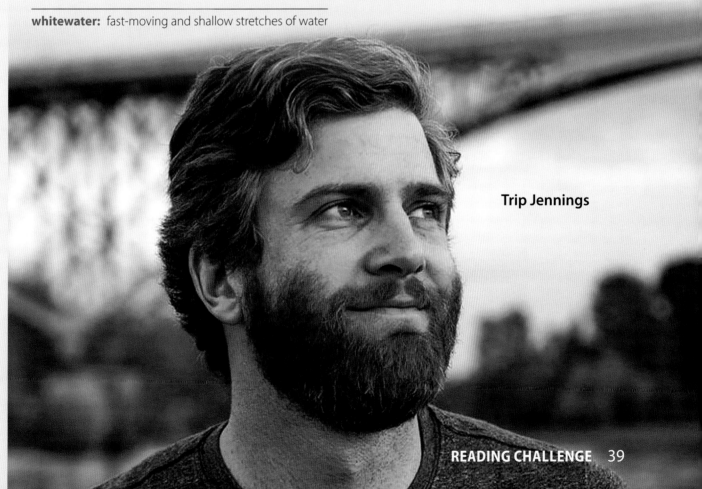

Trip Jennings

2 Personal Finance

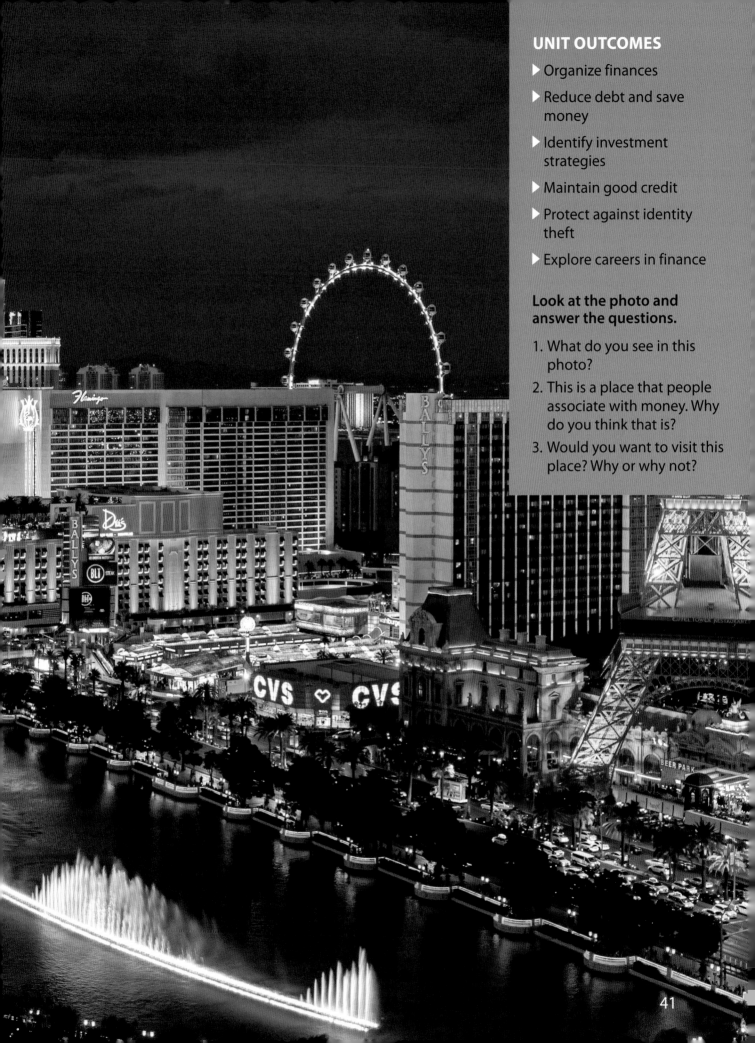

UNIT OUTCOMES

▶ Organize finances

▶ Reduce debt and save money

▶ Identify investment strategies

▶ Maintain good credit

▶ Protect against identity theft

▶ Explore careers in finance

Look at the photo and answer the questions.

1. What do you see in this photo?
2. This is a place that people associate with money. Why do you think that is?
3. Would you want to visit this place? Why or why not?

41

Vocabulary Builder

A Read Kimla's list of financial goals.

1. I need to stop *impulse buying* and pay off my credit cards.

2. I want to stop *living paycheck to paycheck* and save enough money for a down payment on a house.

3. I want to increase my *purchasing power* by putting $200 a month into an emergency savings account.

4. I want us to start *living within our means*, so I can start giving $25 a month to charity.

B INFER What does each italicized expression in **A** mean? Discuss the expressions with your classmates.

C Often, if you try to understand the meaning of the individual words in a new phrase, you can understand the phrase. Try to figure out the meanings of these phrases with a partner.

1. budget cut   2. buy in bulk

3. remote deposit   4. commit fraud

5. electronic payment   6. current income

7. delinquent accounts   8. online banking

9. unauthorized transactions

D Work with a partner. Choose three expressions from **C** and make sentences.

Life ONLINE When you need to pay a friend or family or even a business and you don't have cash on you, you can use an app on your phone to send them money from your bank. Do you use any apps like these? If so, which ones?

E **INFER** Read the sentences. Try to figure out the meanings of the underlined words.

1. The company declared <u>bankruptcy</u> when it ran out of money.

   Bankruptcy means _____.

2. I took out a loan at the bank and used my house as <u>collateral</u>.

   Collateral means _____.

3. The thought of starting a business was <u>daunting</u>, but he decided to do it anyway.

   Daunting means _____.

4. <u>Inflation</u> was so great that bread cost twice as much in June as it did in May.

   Inflation means _____.

5. His <u>investment</u> in the stock market has made him a millionaire.

   Investment means _____.

6. The company has no <u>liquid</u> assets; therefore, it can't pay its bills.

   Liquid means _____.

7. The <u>penalty</u> for filing my income tax late was a fine.

   Penalty means _____.

8. He <u>periodically</u> reviews his budget and makes changes when necessary.

   Periodically means _____.

9. Investing money in the stock market might be <u>risky</u> because you could lose it.

   Risky means _____.

F Look back at Kimla's financial goals in **A**. Using some of the phrases from **C**, write four of your own financial goals.

1. _____

2. _____

3. _____

4. _____

Getting Organized

GOAL ▶ Organize finances

A Look back at the goals you wrote in **F**. Rewrite your financial goals, giving each one a time frame.

By the end of next year, I will have paid off my credit cards.

1. _____

2. _____

3. _____

4. _____

B **CALCULATE** Think about how you spend your money. Answer the questions on a separate piece of paper.

1. Did you go on vacation last year? How much did it cost?

2. How much do you spend during the holidays or on family birthdays every year?

3. How often do you get your hair cut? How much does it cost?

4. What do you spend on transportation each month? Do you have a bus pass, ride a bike, drive a car?

C Listen to a financial planner talking about how to organize personal finances. Write down the most important points. 🎧

1. _____

2. _____

3. _____

4. _____

5. _____

D Compare your notes in **C** with a partner. Add any important points you missed.

E **ANALYZE** After meeting with a financial planner, Kimla and her husband looked at all of their bank statements, credit card statements, ATM records, and receipts. Look at the spreadsheet that they created. What do they still need to calculate?

MONEY OUT		
	Annual	Monthly
Mortgage / Rent	_____	$2,200
Home maintenance	_____	$250
Renters' insurance	$1,200	_____
Gas / Electric	_____	$225
Water	_____	$70
Phone	_____	$130
Food / Restaurants	_____	$500
Medical / Dental	_____	$145
Auto expenses	_____	$450
Tolls / Fares / Parking	_____	$120
Clothes / Shoes	$1,200	_____
Dry cleaning	_____	$45
Hair / Manicure / Facial	_____	$75
Kids' school / Sports	$1,800	_____
Training / Education	$300	_____
Income taxes	$23,150	_____
Internet	_____	$50
Credit cards / Loans	_____	$850
Subscriptions	$48	_____
Entertainment	_____	$125
Cable / Streaming	_____	$150
Vacations	$2,100	_____
Hobbies	$180	_____
Gifts	$800	_____
TOTAL	_____	_____

Calculations

To calculate annual expenses, multiply monthly expenses by 12:

250	15	55	1300
$\times 12$	$\times 12$	$\times 12$	$\times 12$
3000	180		

To calculate monthly expenses, divide annual expenses by 12:

$3000 \div 12 = 250$ $180 \div 12 = 15$

_____ $\div 12 = 55$ _____ $\div 12 = 1300$

F Calculate Kimla and her husband's annual and monthly totals.

G Together, Kimla and her husband make $97,375 annually before deductions. Answer the questions.

1. How much do they have left over annually?

   _____

2. How much do they have left over each month?

   _____

3. Do you think Kimla and her husband live within their means? Why?

   _____

H In the spreadsheet in **E**, some expenses are *fixed* (stay the same every month) and others are *variable* (change from month to month). With a partner, make a list of Kimla and her husband's fixed and variable expenses.

Fixed	Variable

I Look back at Kimla's financial goals in **A** in Vocabulary Builder. How much money does she want to start saving each month for emergencies and giving to charity? Does she have enough in her budget for these items? If not, which expenses do you think Kimla and her husband can cut back on?

J Make a spreadsheet like the one in **E**, listing all your monthly and annual expenses. Next to each expense, write *f* for a fixed expense or *v* for a variable expense. Look at the spreadsheet to get you started.

	Annual	Monthly
Mortgage / Rent (f)		
Home maintenance (v)		
Gas / Electric (v)		
Water (v)		

Managing Money

GOAL ▶ Reduce debt and save money

A Read the ad. 🎧

Too Much Debt?

Do you live within your means or do you live paycheck to paycheck?

Do you owe money to a bank or another person?

We Can Help!

The first thing we will help you do is make a budget. It is important to plan out your monthly expenses so you know where your money is going each month. Our advisors will help you get on track so you can make some cuts to your monthly budget. These cuts will allow you to pay off your debt faster. We'll show you how to get rid of bad debt by paying off your higher interest and long-term debts first. We'll help you analyze your credit reports and discuss ways to boost your credit rating. We'll also teach you some helpful tips; here's one: Credit card interest is calculated daily, so if you make your payment earlier than the due date, you'll actually save interest! If there are some debts that you just can't pay, we'll contact the creditors and arrange settlements for you.

How can you afford not to let us help you? **Click here.**

B Answer the questions about the ad with a partner.

1. Who do you think wrote the ad? _____

2. What is the purpose of the ad? _____

3. Would you click on the bottom of the ad? Why? _____

_____

4. The ad mentions different ways to help people reduce debt. List four suggestions.

a. _____

b. _____

c. _____

d. _____

C Read the tips on how to save money. 🎧

Tips For Saving Money

- Avoid impulse buying.
- Shop for bargains, not designer labels.
- Buy a used car instead of a new one.
- Buy generic products rather than brand names.
- Start or join a carpool.
- Think before you buy: *Do I really need this?*
- Buy groceries at the market, not the convenience store.
- Increase your insurance deductible.
- Make meals at home instead of eating out.

- Make your own coffee in the morning.
- Pay your credit card in full each month to avoid paying interest.
- Plan ahead for food purchases so you can buy in bulk.
- Shop around for the best prices.
- Turn the heat temperature down in the winter and the air-conditioning temperature up in the summer.
- Check price comparison sites.
- Use a money-saving app.
- Use a budgeting app or spreadsheet.

D ANALYZE Do you already follow some of the tips in **C**? Choose the ones you are familiar with. Underline the ones you would like to follow in the future.

E Listen to Kimla and her husband, Samir, talk about saving money. Write *T* if a statement is true or *F* if a statement is false. 🎧

1. Kimla buys designer clothes. _____

2. Samir had been buying his coffee at a coffee shop. _____

3. Kimla had been paying high interest on credit cards. _____

4. Samir had been looking at new cars. _____

5. Kimla turns off the air conditioner before she goes to bed. _____

6. Samir called the insurance company to increase their deductible. _____

7. Kimla has never bought generic products. _____

8. Samir collects coupons. _____

F Study the chart.

Past Perfect Continuous					
First Event in Past					**Second Event in Past**
Subject	*had*	*been*	**Verb + -ing**		
Kimla	had	been	buying	designer clothes	before she started bargain hunting.
Samir	had	been	buying	coffee at a coffee shop	before he began making it at home.
They	had	been	paying	a lower deductible	before they called the insurance company.

Uses
- We use the past perfect continuous to talk about an activity that was happening for a while before another event happened in the past. For the more recent event, we use the simple past.
- Remember to use a comma if you begin the sentence with the second event. *Before she started bargain hunting, Kimla had been buying designer clothes.*

G Think about your past behavior and how you have changed it to reduce debt and save money. Write four statements.

I had been eating out for lunch every day before I started making my lunch at home.

1. _____

2. _____

3. _____

4. _____

H Write four ways in which you can change your behavior to reduce debt and save money.

Tomorrow, I will start making my lunch at home.

1. _____

2. _____

3. _____

4. _____

Investing Wisely

GOAL ▶ Identify investment strategies

A In a small group, look at the words and phrases. Write your own definition for those you know. Find the meanings of those you don't know.

capital gains	inflation	net appreciation	purchasing power	value
convert	liquid	penalty	risky	vehicle

B **COMPARE** Look at your meaning for *vehicle*. Is it the same as this definition?

vehicle *n.* a way in which something is accomplished

C **PREDICT** Based on the words and phrases you defined in **A**, what do you think the article in **D** is about? Discuss your ideas with your classmates.

D Read the article about investing money.

Due to inflation, money is worth less and less each year, so by not investing your money, you are actually losing money. In order to prevent inflation from destroying the value of your money, you should invest. Let's take a look at some basic kinds of investments.

An investment can make you money in three basic ways. First, an investment can earn current income. *Current income* is money that you receive periodically, for example, every month or every six months. An example of an investment that provides current income is a certificate of deposit (CD) because interest is paid to your account periodically. A second way that an investment can make money is through *capital growth*. This is when the amount of money you have invested grows in value over time. When you sell the investment,

you get your money back plus any increase in value. Examples of capital growth investments are stocks and other assets that you own, such as your home. Finally, a third way that an investment can earn income is through a combination of current income and capital growth. Examples include rental property and stocks that pay *dividends*, that is, extra or bonus amounts of money.

There are many different ways to invest your money, but let's look at five of the most widely used investment vehicles.

Probably the most popular investment vehicle is the savings account, which offers low minimum deposits, liquidity (the ability to withdraw and deposit whenever you want), and insurance protection. Because of these features, savings accounts pay relatively low interest rates. Another investment vehicle that is somewhat similar to a savings account in that it offers insurance protection and low interest rates is a certificate of deposit (CD). A CD requires that you put money in and leave it for a certain amount of time—three months, six months, a year, etc. Usually, the longer the amount of time you keep it in, the higher the interest. CDs are not perfectly liquid because early withdrawal of funds from a CD often results in a penalty. Another type of investment is a mutual fund where a number of investors put their money together to buy specific investments. Some mutual funds invest in stocks, some in bonds, and some in real estate. The mutual fund investor owns shares of the fund, not the actual stocks, bonds, or property purchased by the fund. Most likely, when a person thinks of investing, he or she probably thinks of the stock market. Ownership of a stock represents ownership of a *claim* on the net earnings of a company. Therefore, stock earnings depend on how well the company is doing. Stocks can be quickly converted to cash by selling them on the stock market, but because the price of stocks changes daily, there is no guarantee that you will get back the money that you paid for the stock. And finally, property or real estate is a popular investment because it can produce returns in two ways: current income and net appreciation (capital gains). You can receive current income if the property is used, such as in situations where tenants are renting it or if crops are grown on the land. Net appreciation occurs if the property increases in value during the time that you own it. A major disadvantage of real estate and rental property is that they are not very liquid; it takes time and resources to turn them into cash. It may take many months to sell a piece of property.

So, which investment will be best for you? Only you can decide. Think carefully about your financial situation, how much money you can or want to invest, and how soon you will need access to the money.

E **Discuss these questions with a partner.**

1. Do you invest your money? If so, how do you invest it?

2. What investment vehicles would you like to try?

3. Would you say you are conservative with your money? Why or why not?

F Use the ideas you have learned about investment strategies in this lesson to complete the sentences. Each sentence may have more than one answer.

1. If you invest your money, you can _____ it over time.

2. The _____ of stocks is based on the earnings of the company.

3. Savings accounts and mutual funds are not very _____.

4. It is not easy to _____ real estate into cash.

5. Savings accounts are very _____. You can get the cash whenever you need it.

6. My favorite investment _____ is _____ (your own idea).

G Read the article in **D** again and complete the outline.

   I. Inflation

     A. _____

  II. Investments make you money.

     A. *Current income (CDs)*

     B. _____

     C. _____

 III. Popular investment types

     A. _____

     B. _____

     C. *Stocks*

     D. _____

     E. _____

H SUMMARIZE On a separate piece of paper, write a one-paragraph summary of the article in **D** using the notes from your outline in **G**.

Credit

GOAL ▶ Maintain good credit

A **In a small group, discuss the questions.**

1. What is credit?

2. What makes credit good or bad?

3. How can you find out if you have good or bad credit?

4. If you have bad credit, how can you improve it?

B **Read the article. Underline the main ideas.** 🎧

The Four Keys to Great Credit

Your credit history can make or break you when trying to convince lenders you're a good risk. Here's how to build the best record you can—before you need it.

Open checking and savings accounts. Having bank accounts establishes you as part of the financial mainstream. Lenders want to know you have a checking account available to pay bills, and a savings account indicates you're putting aside something for the future.

Get your credit report—if you have one. Next, you need to find out how lenders view you. Most lenders base their decisions on credit reports, which are compiled by companies known as credit bureaus. You are entitled to a free credit report from each of the three major bureaus each

year. Typically, a credit report includes identifying information about you, such as your name, address, social security number, and birth date. The report may also list any credit accounts or loans opened in your name, along with your payment history, account limits, and unpaid balances.

Fix any errors or omissions. Some credit reports include errors— accounts that don't belong to you or that include out-of-date or misleading information. You should read through each of your three reports and note anything that's incorrect. Negative information, such as late payments, delinquencies, liens, and judgments against you, should be dropped after seven years. A bankruptcy can stay on your report for up to ten years.

(continued)

Add positive information to your report. The more information you can provide about yourself, the more comfortable lenders may feel extending credit to you. Here's a list of items to consider:

- Are your employer and your job title listed?
- Is your address listed and correct?
- Is your social security number listed and correct?
- Is your telephone number listed and correct?
- Does your report include all the accounts you've paid on time?

Establish credit. There are three common routes for establishing new credit:

1. Apply for department store and gasoline cards. These are usually easier to get than major bank credit cards.
2. Consider taking out a small personal loan from your local bank or credit union and paying the money back over time. The bank may require you to put up some collateral—such as the same amount you're borrowing, deposited into a savings account.
3. Apply for a secured credit card. These work like the loan described above: You deposit a certain amount at a bank, and in return you're given a Visa or MasterCard with a credit limit roughly equal to the amount you deposited.

Once you've got credit, use it correctly. Charge small amounts on each card—but never more than you can pay off each month. You need to use credit regularly to establish your credit history, but there's usually no advantage to paying interest on those charges. Once you've been approved for one card or loan, don't rush out and apply for several more. Applying for too much credit will hurt, rather than help, your credit.

C **Imagine you are a financial advisor. Write advice based on the questions. Then share your advice with a partner.**

1. What can I do to establish good credit?

_____

_____

2. What should I look for in my credit report?

_____

_____

3. How can I add positive information to my credit report?

_____

_____

D With a partner, read the article in **B** again and underline six words or phrases you do not understand. Find out their meanings and then write a sentence with each one.

1. _____

2. _____

3. _____

4. _____

5. _____

6. _____

E On a separate piece of paper, write an outline of the article in **B**. Then write a summary.

F Think about your own credit. What are four things you need to do to help establish or maintain your credit?

1. _____

   _____

2. _____

   _____

3. _____

   _____

4. _____

   _____

Identity Theft

GOAL ▶ Protect against identity theft

A Listen to three people talk about their financial problems. What happened in each case? Take notes below each photo.

1. _____

2. _____

3. _____

B Have you ever had a problem similar to the ones in **A**? If so, what did you do about it? Tell your classmates.

C In a small group, discuss the questions.

1. What is identity theft?

2. Are you familiar with the words *smishing, skimming, phishing*, and *vishing*? What do you think they mean?

3. What are some things a person who steals your identity might do? Come up with some ideas in addition to the three in **A**.

4. What can you do if someone steals your identity?

Life ONLINE

One of the more common ways to steal a person's identity today is through fake websites. A fake website can look almost exactly like the real website which makes people more likely to provide their personal information.

To check that a website is legitimate:
1. Double check the URL. A fake website may have one different letter or maybe the wrong domain (.net instead of .com).
2. Look for the lock 🔒 to make sure the website is encrypted, or secure.

D Listen to an interview with a member of the Federal Trade Commission (FTC). In each question, one answer is NOT correct. Choose the incorrect answer.

1. What is identity theft?

   a. when someone uses your credit card number without permission to buy things

   b. when someone steals your name and social security number to commit crimes

   c. when someone commits fraud using your personal information

   d. when someone asks you for your personal information

2. What are some ways thieves steal your identity?

   a. phishing   b. stealing

   c. changing your name   d. skimming

3. An example of bank fraud is . . .

   a. when someone takes out a loan in your name.

   b. when someone gets a driver's license in your name.

   c. when someone opens an account in your name.

   d. when someone creates counterfeit checks using your account number.

4. How can you find out if your identity has been stolen?

   a. cancel credit card accounts

   b. monitor bank accounts

   c. check credit reports

   d. check bank statements

5. What should you do if your identity has been stolen?

   a. notify creditors   b. file a police report

   c. try to find the thief   d. check credit reports

6. How can you help fight identity theft?

   a. educate friends and family about identity theft

   b. be aware of how information is stolen

   c. monitor personal information

   d. donate money to the Federal Trade Commission

E SUMMARIZE Using the information in D, work with a group to write a summary about identify theft.

_____

_____

_____

_____

_____

_____

_____

_____

_____

_____

_____

_____

_____

F In your group, use your summary to prepare a presentation that will educate your classmates about identity theft. Answer the questions.

1. What information will you present to the class? _____

_____

_____

2. How will you present your information? (orally only, orally and visually, etc.)

_____

3. Who will present which part of the information? (Everyone in your group must participate.)

_____

_____

Explore the Workforce

GOAL ▶ Explore careers in finance

A Look at the list of common financial careers. What do you think each person does? Brainstorm and make notes with a partner.

Career	Job Description	Median Salary
Accountant		
Actuary		
Credit Analyst		
Financial Analyst		
Financial Planner		
Stock Trader		

B Listen to a career counselor advise a student who is thinking about a career in finance. Adjust your job descriptions and fill in the median salary information. 🎧

C List the careers in order from the highest salary to the lowest salary.

1. _____   2. _____

3. _____   4. _____

5. _____   6. _____

D Of the careers in **A**, which one sounds the most interesting to you? Why?

_____

_____

_____

E There are a few different areas where people with finance experience can work. Look at the pie chart and answer the questions.

Finance Jobs by Sector

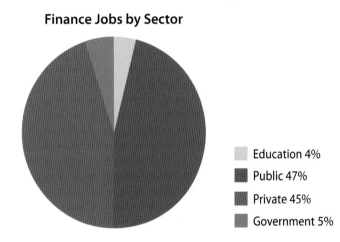

Education 4%
Public 47%
Private 45%
Government 5%

Public Company vs. Private Company

A public company is publicly traded on the stock exchange which means individual investors can own a piece of the company. A private company is owned by one or a few individuals.

1. Where are the best job opportunities for a finance professional?

   a. government   b. education   c. private companies   d. public companies

2. Where should you NOT go looking for a job if you need one right away?

   a. private companies   b. public companies

   c. schools   d. none of the above

F Create a pie chart with the data. Add a legend.

Bachelor's 77%
Master's 11%
Associate 8%
High School Diploma 1%
Other Degrees 3%

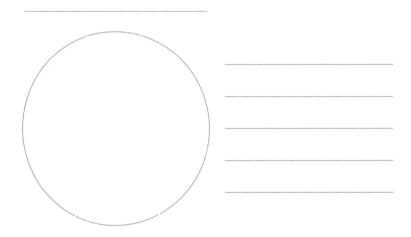

G What do you think the best title for your pie chart would be? Write it above the graph.

H What skills are needed for careers in finance? Discuss the terms in the box and try to figure out what each one means.

communication skills	strong analytical skills
critical thinking skills	strong communication skills
detail-oriented	strong decision-making skills
entrepreneurial mindset	strong interpersonal skills
interpersonal skills	strong problem-solving skills
research skills	strong reasoning skills

I Think about what you know about the finance careers and write the skills you think are needed for each career.

Career	Skills Needed
Accountant	
Actuary	
Credit Analyst	
Financial Analyst	
Financial Planner	
Stock Trader	

J **REFLECT** In your notebook, write the skills from **H** that you have.

K What skills would you like to work on? Make a list in your notebook.

Review

A Joao makes $95,000 a year. Complete his spreadsheet with the missing amounts. Then answer the questions.

MONEY OUT		
	Annual	**Monthly**
Rent	_____	$2,200
Home maintenance	_____	$150
Renters' insurance	$1,200	_____
Gas / Electric	_____	$220
Water	_____	$40
Phone	_____	$120
Food / Restaurants	_____	$400
Medical / Dental	_____	$140
Auto expenses	_____	$890
Clothes / Shoes	$1,125	_____
Hair / Manicure / Facial	_____	$125
Training / Education	$700	_____
Income taxes	$17,560	_____
Internet	_____	$75
Credit cards / Loans	_____	$975
Entertainment	_____	$425
Cable / Streaming	_____	$140
Vacations	$2,500	_____
Gifts	$795	_____
TOTAL		

1. How much does he have left over each year? _____

2. How much does he have left over each month? _____

3. Do you think Joao lives within his means? _____

4. What suggestions would you make for cutting his spending?

   a. _____
   _____

   b. _____
   _____

   c. _____
   _____

   d. _____
   _____

B Write four tips for saving money.

1. _____   2. _____

3. _____   4. _____

C Complete each statement with the past perfect continuous and the simple past.

1. Erika _____ _had been buying_ _____ (buy) lunch every day before she
   _____ _started_ _____ (start) making it at home.

Learner Log	I can organize finances.	I can reduce debt and save money.
	☐ Yes ☐ No ☐ Maybe	☐ Yes ☐ No ☐ Maybe

2. Duc _____ (charge) his credit cards to their maximum limits
before he _____ (cut) them up.

3. Before the Ingrams _____ (buy) a new car, they
_____ (lease) a used one.

4. We _____ (live) beyond our means before we
_____ (organize) our finances.

5. Before she _____ (research) insurance rates, she
_____ (spend) too much on auto insurance.

D In your notebook, write four things you have learned about investing. Share your ideas with a partner. Add two ideas that your partner came up with.

E Answer the following questions by yourself or with a partner.

1. What is credit? _____

2. What can you do to establish good credit? _____

3. What makes credit good or bad? _____

4. How can you find out if you have good or bad credit? _____

5. If you have bad credit, how can you improve it? _____

6. What should you look for in your credit report? _____

7. How can you add positive information to your credit report? _____

F Read each scenario. In your notebook, write what you think happened and what the person should do to fix the problem.

1. Marcia tried to withdraw money from her account, which had over $1,000 in it the last time she checked, but the bank said she had insufficient funds.

2. Marco noticed some unfamiliar charges on his credit card statement.

3. The IRS contacted Ekaterina and said she never paid income tax on a second job, which she didn't have.

Learner Log	I can identify investment strategies.			I can maintain good credit.			I can protect against identity theft.		
	Yes	No	Maybe	Yes	No	Maybe	Yes	No	Maybe

Vocabulary Review

A A *synonym* is a word that has the same meaning as another word. Look at the words and choose a synonym from the box.

bargain	counterfeit	delinquent	expense	risk
convert	debt	earnings	fraud	worth

1. income _____

2. fake _____

3. late _____

4. scam _____

5. cost _____

6. good deal _____

7. money due _____

8. liability _____

9. change _____

10. value _____

B Look back in the unit and find three new terms you learned (other than the words in **A**). Write a sentence using each of these terms.

1. _____

2. _____

3. _____

C Complete each sentence with an appropriate word or phrase. In many cases, more than one word or expression will work.

1. There are many ways in which people can steal your identity. Two of them are
   _____ and _____.

2. A safe way to invest your money is by investing in _____.

3. A riskier way to invest is by investing in _____.

4. One good way to establish credit is _____.

5. Another way is _____.

6. If your identity is stolen, you should _____.

Financial Assistance

SOFT SKILL ▶ Collaboration

A These two agencies are run by the government and can give people financial assistance. Discuss the questions with your classmates and teacher.

- FDIC (Federal Deposit Insurance Corporation) Consumers and Communities

- FTC (Federal Trade Commission) Consumer Protection

1. What do the FDIC and the FTC do? How can they help?

B Search the sites of the agencies in **A** for more information. Click on the topics you find interesting in the consumer section of each site. Write what you find.

1. What are some consumer resources on the FDIC website? _____

_____

_____

_____

2. How can you report fraud on the FTC website? _____

_____

_____

C Search each issue and find a website that has the information needed. Write the URL on the line. Then answer each question.

1. impostor scams

   URL: _____
   What is an impostor scam?

2. stopping telemarketing calls

   URL: _____
   How can you stop telemarketers from calling you?

3. unemployment insurance fraud

   URL: _____
   What are the warning signs of an unemployment insurance fraud?

COLLABORATION:
Verify Your Sources

When doing research, it is important to check that the information you are using comes from a reliable source. Here are some tips to keep in mind:

- Check the URL of the site. Sites with ".edu" and ".gov" are generally reliable sources.

- Don't rely solely on individual blogs, online forums or Wikipedia.

- If the data is published by an author, check who they are, what their credentials are, if their opinions are supported by facts, and who their audience is. You can also check the "About Us" section of a site to check for potential conflicts of interest.

Reading Challenge

A **PREDICT** In a group, discuss the words. Which ones are familiar to you? What do they mean?

affiliate marketing	content creator	podcast
blogger	passive income	side hustle

B Complete the statements with one of the words from **A**.

1. She became a _____ that writes about parenting after the birth of her third son.

2. I need to find a _____ so I can make more money.

3. My mom is always listening to financial _____.

4. We are renting the room above our garage to give us some _____.

5. _____ is when you buy something from a link on a person's website, which gives them a commission.

6. Javier is one of the top _____ at his company.

C Read about Jannese Torres and pay special attention when you see vocabulary from **B**. Review **B** and check your answers.

D Choose the best answer.

1. Why did Jannese become an entrepreneur?

   a. She got fired from her job.

   b. She was tired of working for someone else.

   c. She had a lot of student loan debt.

   d. all of the above

2. According to the reading, why did Jannese start a personal finance podcast?

   a. She didn't get into culinary school.

   b. She wanted to generate passive income.

   c. She wanted to share the FIRE concepts that she learned.

   d. She wanted to see more Latinas talking about business.

E What does FIRE mean?

_____

_____

F Find Jannese's podcast and listen to an episode. What did you learn?

Jannese Torres

Yo Quiero Dinero

Jannese Torres is the creator and host of an award-winning podcast about personal finance called *Yo Quiero Dinero*, which translates to *I Want Money*. But as a kid, she did not know anything about money. She had to learn how to manage money as an adult. When she was 25, still in school, and working at a job she hated, she got fired. That experience caused her
5 to rebuild her life. She decided that she wanted freedom from working for someone else. She had always been passionate about food and cooking, so she thought about going to culinary school but realized she would be working for someone else again. So, she learned everything she could about blogging and ended up starting her own business, which turned out to be the beginning of her journey as an entrepreneur.
10 At the time, Jannese owed over $39,000 in student loans, so she figured out how to pay them off by doing side hustles. From listening to podcasts, she had learned about the concept of FIRE (Financial Independence / Retire Early). She wanted to be able to generate passive income but also wanted to find a way to make money doing what she loved. This led her to start her online career as a content creator, more specifically, a food blogger. She began sharing her family
15 recipes on a website and social media, where she was able to make money through sponsored content, affiliate marketing, and display ads, which eventually led her to a six-figure income.

Jannese eventually created her own personal finance platform because she wanted to see more Latinas in podcasting talking about wealth and business. She had been listening to personal finance podcasts for years before she started implementing the FIRE concepts into her
20 finances and became financially independent. She was surprised that everyone didn't know about investing to reach financial freedom, so she decided to create a podcast that she wanted to listen to. And that's how *Yo Quiero Dinero*, a podcast to "start the conversation about building wealth in the Latinx community," was born.

3 Automotive Know-How

UNIT OUTCOMES

▶ Purchase a car
▶ Maintain and repair a car
▶ Interpret an auto insurance policy
▶ Compute mileage, gas consumption, and energy used
▶ Follow the rules of the road
▶ Explore careers in the automotive industry

Look at the photo and answer the questions.

1. What kind of car do you think this is?
2. Where do you think this photo was taken?
3. Do people drive commonly cars like this one where you come from?
4. Would you drive this car, or would you prefer a newer car? Why?

Vocabulary Builder

A Look at the different types of cars. Use words from **B** to label them.

1.

_____

2.

_____

3.

_____

4.

_____

5.

_____

6.

_____

7.

_____

8.

_____

9.

_____

B How would you describe each car? Write your ideas next to each term.

1. two-door coupe: _____

2. four-door sedan: _____

3. convertible: _____

4. minivan: _____

5. sport utility vehicle (SUV): _____

6. sports car: _____

7. station wagon: _____

8. pickup truck: _____

9. van: _____

10. electric: _____

11. hybrid: _____

12. gas: _____

C Here are some words and phrases that you will find in this unit. Replace each verb in bold with a synonym from the box. Some words can be used more than once.

change	choose	commute	do	fill up	find	imagine	look at	replace

1. _____ **Change** your air filter.

2. _____ **Perform** an oil change.

3. _____ **Check** your oil levels.

4. _____ **Pick** your lane and stick with it.

5. _____ **Drive** during off-peak hours.

6. _____ **Pretend** you have a hybrid.

7. _____ **Inspect** your brakes.

8. _____ **Replace** your wipers.

9. _____ **Look for** telecommuting opportunities.

10. _____ **Top off** your washer fluid.

D How are these types of vehicles different? What do they have in common? Brainstorm with a partner and complete the Venn diagram.

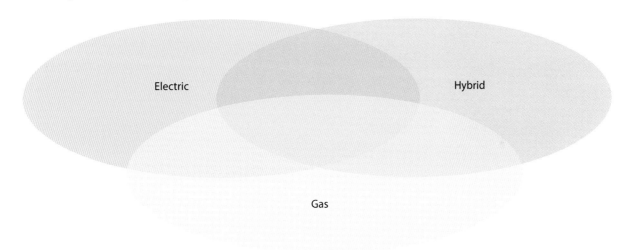

Electric

Hybrid

Gas

E What do the following words have in common? Write the theme.

Theme: _____

_____ accident

_____ coverage

_____ make

_____ premium

_____ bodily injury

_____ incident

_____ model

_____ uninsured motorist

_____ collision

_____ limits of liability

_____ policy

_____ VIN

F Mark the terms you know in E. Walk around the classroom and find classmates who can explain the terms you don't know.

LESSON 1

Buying a Car

GOAL ▶ Purchase a car

A In a group, discuss the following questions.

1. What type of car do you have? (If you don't have a car, think of someone you know who does.)

2. What is the car like? (Ask about color, size, make, model, etc.)

3. How did you get the car?

4. How long have you had the car?

B Listen to an auto salesman who is trying to sell you a car. Take notes on what he says about the different types of cars. 🎧

Vehicle	Best for	Pros	Cons
	most people		
			backseats are hard to access
	active family		
		great in good weather	

C You are going to buy a new or used car. Look back at the table in **B**. Which type of car would be best for you? Why?

_____

_____

_____

_____

D Now that you have an idea which car is best for you, it is a good idea to do some research on your own. What are the best ways to find out more about the car you want to buy? In a group, brainstorm ways to research different car models.

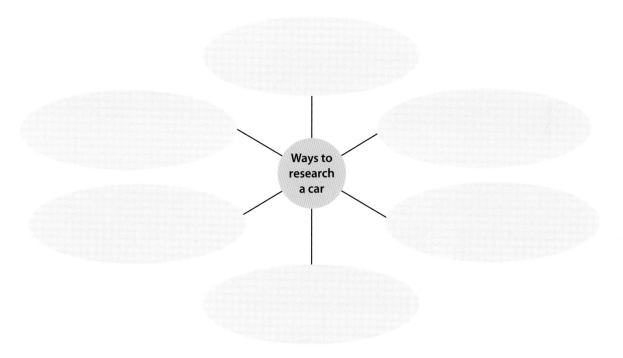

Ways to research a car

E Rachel has decided to buy an electric two-door coupe. Listen and write what she did to research buying her car.

1. _____

2. _____

3. _____

4. _____

5. _____

F To supplement your research, ask different people for their opinions about cars. What are some questions you might ask? With a partner, create a list of questions.

Friends and family

1. _____

2. _____

3. _____

Car dealer

1. _____

2. _____

3. _____

Mechanic

1. _____

2. _____

3. _____

Loan officer

1. _____

2. _____

3. _____

G Make a plan to purchase a car. Write the steps you will take in this plan.

Step 1: _____

_____

Step 2: _____

_____

Step 3: _____

_____

Maintenance and Repair

GOAL ▶ Maintain and repair a car

A With your teacher's help, identify the auto parts in the box. Then label the picture.

air filter	distributor	rear axle
alternator	exhaust manifold	rear suspension
battery	fuel injection system	timing belt
brake fluid reservoir	muffler	water pump
coolant reservoir	power steering reservoir	
disc brake	radiator	

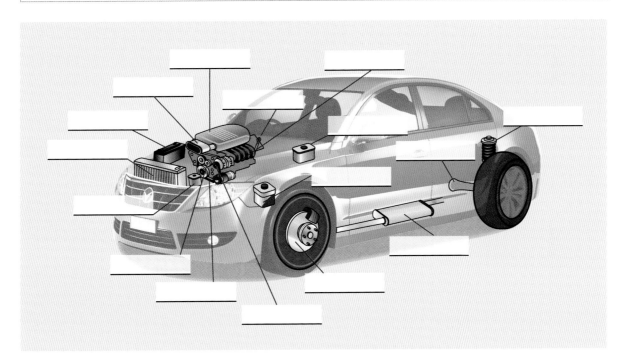

B What is the purpose of each auto part in **A**? Work with a partner and use a dictionary to define each part on a separate sheet of paper. Share your answers with other pairs.

C Now that you are more familiar with auto parts and their importance, read this excerpt from an auto maintenance and repair guide. 🎧

How to Maintain Your Automobile

Change your air filter. A clogged air filter can affect your gas mileage as well as the performance of your engine. Change it on a regular basis.

Check your oil levels. Your engine needs a certain amount of oil to run properly, so it's important to check the oil levels regularly.

Perform an oil change. As your engine uses oil, the oil becomes dirty and should be changed at regular intervals.

Perform a timing belt inspection. A faulty timing belt can result in bent valves and other expensive engine damage. Check it at least every 10,000 miles, and replace it when the manufacturer recommends doing so.

Replace your wipers. Windshield wipers can wear out, and if they aren't working properly, they could impair your vision while on the road. Change them at least twice a year.

Perform a radiator flush. It's important to keep your radiator and cooling system clean.

Check your power steering fluid. Check your power steering fluid regularly to make sure your power steering doesn't fail.

Inspect your brakes. Protect yourself and your passengers by inspecting your brakes twice a year.

Check and fill your coolant. If your car is low on coolant, it will run hot, so make sure to check the coolant level in your radiator.

Check and replace your spark plugs. A faulty spark plug could cause poor gas mileage or a rough running engine and poor acceleration. Make sure to replace the spark plugs as recommended by your car's manual.

Top off your washer fluid. Make sure you have enough washer fluid so you can keep your windshield clean.

Check your wheel bolts. Check the tightness of your wheel bolts on a regular basis to make sure there is no danger of your wheels becoming loose.

D With a partner, answer these questions on a separate piece of paper.

1. What fluids need to be regularly checked?

2. Why is it important to replace windshield wipers?

3. Why is it bad to have a clogged air filter?

4. Why should you inspect your timing belt?

5. Why should you check your wheel bolts?

6. What could happen if you don't have enough power steering fluid?

E Some people can perform their own maintenance while others need the help of trained professionals. Who will do your car repairs? If you need help, how will you find a reliable mechanic? Read the guide. 🎧

Guide to Getting Repairs Done

1. Ask a friend, relative, or coworker for recommendations when looking for a good auto shop or mechanic. Also, take time to find a local garage that you feel comfortable with.
2. Make a list of services you need performed or the symptoms your vehicle is experiencing so there is no misunderstanding.
3. Get more than one opinion about the repairs that need to be done.
4. Ask for a written estimate before the job is started.
5. Get more than one estimate and compare prices.
6. Ask about the warranty policy.
7. Have the mechanic show you what you need replaced and ask why you need to replace it.
8. Go for a test drive in your car before paying for the repairs. If something is not right with the repairs, make it understood that you are not happy. Do not pay the bill until the vehicle is repaired properly.
9. Pay with a credit card. Many credit cards offer consumer protection for fraud.
10. If you discover something is not fixed after you've paid and driven home, call the garage and explain the situation. Go back to the garage as soon as possible.

F Write the numbers 1 to 10 on a separate piece of paper. Close your books and see how many suggestions from **E** you can remember. Write them down.

G Make an outline for each of the guides in **C** and **E**.

H SUMMARIZE Using your outlines, write a two-paragraph summary of what you have learned in this lesson. Remember to format your paragraphs correctly.

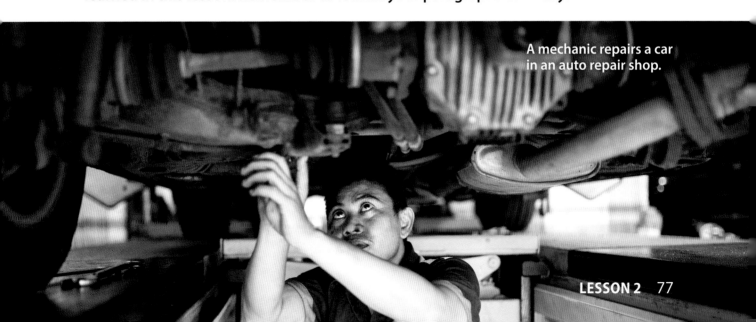

A mechanic repairs a car in an auto repair shop.

Car Insurance

GOAL ▶ Interpret an auto insurance policy

A **Discuss these questions with your classmates.**

1. Do you drive a car or ride a motorbike?

2. Do you have insurance?

3. Why is it important to have auto insurance?

4. Do you understand your insurance policy?

5. Is it against the law in your state to drive without insurance?

B **Read what each person says about auto insurance policies. Discuss the meanings of the words in bold with a partner.**

"An insurance **policy** is a contract between you and the insurance company that states what the company will pay for in the event of an accident." — **Chalene**

"The insurance **premium** is the amount you pay for auto insurance for a certain period of time." — **Keona**

"**Coverage** is what is included in the insurance—what the company will pay for." — **Binata**

C **Look at Chalene's policy and find each of the items.**

⭐ Bright Star Insurance

Name of Insured and Address: Chalene Johnson 24573 Thatch Street Houston, TX 77042	Policy Number: 05XX 52 870 1625 Q Policy Period: Effective Jan 13, 2023 to Jul 13, 2023
Description of Vehicle(s) **Year and Make:** 2019 Cury **VIN:** QXXPYR18924G23794	**Annual Mileage:** 9,000 **Premium for this Policy Period:** $526.04

Coverage	Limits of Liability	Six-Month Premium
A. Bodily Injury	Each Person $100,000; Each Accident $300,000	$197.65
B. Collision	Each Accident $50,000	$178.56
C. Comprehensive	Each Incident $25,000	$75.41
D. Uninsured Motor Vehicle Bodily Injury	Each Person $50,000; Each Accident $150,000	$74.42
E. Physical Damage	Deductible $1,000	
		TOTAL $526.04

1. Policy number: _____

2. VIN: _____

3. Policy premium: _____

4. Annual mileage: _____

5. Deductible: _____

6. Make of vehicle: _____

D MATCH There are different types of coverage listed on insurance policies. Match each type of coverage with what it covers.

Coverage	What It Covers
_____ 1. bodily injury liability	a. damage caused by another vehicle without insurance
_____ 2. property damage liability	b. damage to your vehicle due to an auto accident
_____ 3. collision	c. loss or damage to your vehicle or the vehicle you are driving for an incident other than collision (theft, fire, etc.)
_____ 4. medical payments	d. other people's bodily injuries or death for which you are responsible
_____ 5. uninsured motorist's property damage	e. bodily injuries to you or your passengers caused by the accident
_____ 6. uninsured motorist's bodily injury	f. bodily injury caused by another vehicle without insurance
_____ 7. comprehensive	g. damage to another vehicle or property

E With a partner, read each scenario and decide which coverage would apply.

1. Chalene accidentally ran into a tree and damaged the front end of her car. Which type of coverage would apply? _____

2. Binata was driving home from school when she hit another car. She had run through a red light, so the accident was her fault. There was no real damage to her car, but she hurt her back and had to go to the chiropractor. Also, there was significant damage to the car she hit. Which types of coverage would apply? _____

3. Keona and his friend Chalene were driving to the beach when a car hit them from behind. Then, the driver left without giving them any information. Neither Keona nor Chalene was hurt, but there was damage to Keona's car. Which type of coverage would apply?

_____

4. Keona's car got stolen from the parking lot at a movie theater. Which type of coverage would apply? _____

F Look at Chalene's policy in **C**. Write a question for each answer.

EXAMPLE: Chalene Johnson: _Who is being insured through this policy?_

1. $178.56: _____

2. $1,000: _____

3. 05XX 52 870 1625 Q: _____

4. 2019 Cury: _____

5. $526.04: _____

6. 9,000: _____

G Look at Keona's insurance policy and choose the correct answers.

United Automobile Association · Dallas, TX

STATE: TX POLICY NUMBER: QQP15 26 49L3798 1 POLICY PERIOD: September 5th, 2023 to March 5, 2024 VEHICLE(S): 2020 Tallaros, 2022 Rockland	NAME AND ADDRESS OF INSURED: Keona lu 54 Plover Plaza Galveston, TX 50472

Limits of Liability		6-Month Premium
LIABILITY		
Bodily Injury	Each Person $100,000; Each Accident $300,000	$248.52
Property Damage	Each Accident $50,000	$175.26
UNINSURED MOTORISTS		
Bodily Injury	Each Person $100,000; Each Accident $300,000	$110.21
Property Damage	Each Accident $50,000	$98.26
PHYSICAL DAMAGE		
Comprehensive Loss	Deductible $1,000	$125.56
Collision Loss	Deductible $1,000	$165.25
	TOTAL:	$923.06

1. How many vehicles are covered by this policy?

   a. 1   b. 2   c. 3   d. 4

2. Where does the insured motorist live?

   a. Dallas   b. Lake Tahoe   c. Galveston   d. Houston

3. How much is United Automobile Association charging for liability?

   a. $248.52   b. $125.56   c. $175.26   d. $423.78

4. What is Keona's deductible for comprehensive loss?

   a. $165.25   b. $125.56   c. $1,000   d. $50,000

Going the Distance

GOAL ▶ Compute mileage, gas consumption, and energy used

A **Read and listen to the conversation between Keona and Chalene.** 🎧

Keona: I can't believe the price of gasoline! I've been spending almost $100 just to fill up my tank.

Chalene: Same here. I've been trying to figure out how I can use my car less so I save some money on gas.

Keona: Any good ideas?

Chalene: Well, I'm going to start carpooling to school two days a week, which should help. And I'm trying to combine my errands, so I only go out once a week.

Keona: That sounds good. I think I'm going to look into public transportation. I have a long drive to work, so maybe I can figure out how to take the train into town. I'll have to drive to the station and park, but at least I won't be driving all the way to work.

Chalene: That's a great idea! I may look into getting an electric car.

B **Can you think of some other measures Keona and Chalene can take so they won't have to use their cars so much? Write your ideas.**

_____

_____

C **Keona wanted to see his gas mileage, so he checked the display in his car. How do you think Keona might calculate his gas mileage in miles per gallon (mpg)? Create a formula and fill in the *MPG* column in the table.**

Formula: _____

Date	Odometer	Trip	Gallons	MPG
8/7	12,200	245 miles	13	
8/15	12,475	275	14	
8/24	12,760	285	15	
9/1	13,020	260	14.5	

D CALCULATE If gas costs $5.85 per gallon, how much would the gas for each trip in **C** cost?

E In order to improve your gas mileage, you can follow certain maintenance tips. Listen and write the five tips you hear. 🎧

1. _____
2. _____
3. _____
4. _____
5. _____

F How will each of the tips in **E** help? Listen again and write the reasons. 🎧

1. _____
2. _____
3. _____
4. _____
5. _____

G Keona followed the tips. Look at his log and calculate the mpg and cost per mile. Did his mpg improve?

Date	Odometer	Trip	Gallons	MPG	Cost per Gallon	Cost per Mile
10/5	14,687	275 miles	13		$3.05	
10/17	14,962	295 miles	14		$3.07	
10/30	15,262	300 miles	15		$2.95	
11/9	15,542	280 miles	14.5		$3.10	

H ANALYZE Look at the *Cost per Mile* column in **G**. Which week was the cheapest? On a separate piece of paper, write ideas about how Keona can spend less per mile on gas.

I Chalene is considering buying an electric car to save money on gas. With a partner define these terms:

1. kWh: _____

2. battery range (of your vehicle): _____

3. battery capacity: _____

J **CALCULATE** Complete the table. To calculate how many miles per kWh your car gets, you need to divide the battery range by the battery capacity.

expected miles per kWh = battery range ÷ battery capacity

For example, if your EV has a range of 200 miles and the battery capacity is 40 kWh, you should be able to go 5 miles per kWh.

Battery Capacity	EV Range	Miles per kWh
40 kWh	200	5
60 kWh	240	
80 kWh	280	
100 kWh	320	

K In **E**, you listened to tips for improving gas mileage. What tips would apply to an electric vehicle as well?

1. _____   2. _____

L Listen for eight tips on improving efficiency in an EV. Write them.

1. _____

2. _____

3. _____

4. _____

5. _____

6. _____

7. _____

8. _____

M In a small group, write the pros and cons of owning an electric vehicle.

Traffic Laws

GOAL ▶ Follow the rules of the road

A What does each of the following signs mean? Work with a partner.

1.

_____

2.

_____

3.

_____

4.

_____

5.

_____

6.

_____

7.

_____

8.

_____

9.

_____

10.

_____

11.

_____

12.

_____

13.

_____

14.

_____

15.

_____

16.

_____

B Think about the traffic laws you are familiar with. In a small group, write a law for each item.

1. yellow light: _You must slow down at a yellow light._____

2. speed limit: _____

3. seat belts: _____

4. red light: _____

5. children: _____

6. pedestrians: _____

7. stop sign: _____

8. police officer: _____

9. school bus: _____

C The United States Department of Transportation has an organization called the National Highway Traffic Safety Administration (NHTSA) whose mission is to "save lives, prevent injuries, and reduce vehicle-related crashes." Read the data from a study the NHTSA conducted and answer the questions.

Seat Belt Use in the United States 2014–2019						
	2014	**2015**	**2016**	**2017**	**2018**	**2019**
AL	95.7%	93.3%	92%	92.9%	91.8%	92.3%
AK	88.4%	89.3%	88.5%	90.1%	91.6%	94.1%
CA	97.1%	97.3%	96.5%	96.2%	95.9%	97.2%
GA	97.3%	97.3%	97.2%	97.1%	96.3%	95.9%
FL	80.8%	89.4%	89.6%	90.2%	90.6%	89.8%
IL	94.1%	95.2%	93.0%	93.8%	94.6%	94.3%
MA	76.6%	74.1%	78.2%	73.7%	81.6%	81.6%
NY	90.6%	92.2%	91.8%	93.4%	92.9%	94.2%
TX	90.7%	90.5%	91.6%	91.9%	91.3%	90.9%
WA	94.5%	94.6%	94.7%	94.8%	93.2%	93.1%

1. What percentage of drivers wore seat belts in California in 2017? _____96.2%_____

2. Which state had the highest percentage of seat belt use in 2019? _____

3. What percentage of people in Massachusetts wore seat belts in 2019? _____

4. What is the percentage difference in seat belt use between 2016 and 2017 for drivers in Alaska? _____

5. What percentage of drivers wore seat belts in Florida in 2015? _____

D With a partner, make statements about the data in the chart in **C.**

EXAMPLE: _94.8% of drivers in Washington wore seat belts in 2017._

E What are the driving laws regarding alcohol in your state? Discuss them with your class and write them.

_____

_____

_____

F Read the facts on alcohol-related accidents. Choose the ones that are the most surprising to you.

☐ Alcohol-related motor vehicle crashes kill someone every 45 minutes.

☐ In 2020, 11,654 people were killed in alcohol-impaired driving crashes, accounting for 30% of all traffic-related deaths in the United States.

☐ Alcohol-impaired drivers account for 62% of the people who died in alcohol-related crashes in 2020.

☐ A study of 4,243 drivers who were seriously injured in crashes, indicated that 54% of those drivers were under the influence of alcohol and / or drugs other than alcohol (e.g., marijuana, sedatives, and opioids) from September 2019 to July 2021.

☐ In 2020, 229 children ages 14 and younger died in alcohol-impaired driving crashes. This is 21% of traffic-related deaths among children in that age group.

G With a partner, rewrite the facts in **F** in your own words on a separate piece of paper.

EXAMPLE: _Someone is killed every forty-five minutes due to a car accident involving alcohol._

H In a small group, make a list of five driving rules that you all think are the most important. Present your list to the class.

1. _____

2. _____

3. _____

4. _____

5. _____

Life ONLINE

Distracted driving is another risk factor for both drivers and pedestrians. Texting, using a navigation system, and talking on the phone while driving are some examples of distracted driving. Many states have laws that make it illegal to use—or even hold—a phone while driving. To avoid putting yourself and others at risk, keep your full attention on the road when you are at the wheel. Do not multitask while driving. If you need to make a call, text someone, or send an email, do it before your trip, when you find a safe place to stop, or when you get to your destination.

Explore the Workforce

GOAL ▶ Explore careers in the automotive industry

A These are 15 common careers in the automotive industry. Choose each one that you have heard of. Then talk to a partner about what each person does.

☐ Auto body repair technician   ☐ Car rental agent

☐ Auto designer   ☐ Car salesperson

☐ Auto electrician   ☐ Process engineer

☐ Auto engineer   ☐ Quality testing engineer

☐ Auto instructor   ☐ Tire technician

☐ Auto mechanic   ☐ Tow truck driver

☐ Auto sales manager   ☐ Vehicle inspector

☐ Car detailer

B Write a definition for each word.

Manufacturing: _____

Sales: _____

Service: _____

C **CATEGORIZE** Write each job title from **A** under its correct category. Some jobs may fit in more than one category.

Manufacturing	Sales	Service

D Can you think of any other jobs in the automotive industry? Write them in the correct column in **C**.

E One of the most common jobs is auto mechanic. Complete the text with the words in the box. Pay attention to the missing parts of speech (noun, verb, adjective, etc.) to help you.

auto body shops	mathematics	software
dealership	mechanics	specialize in
heavy machinery	minimum requirement	technical education
inspecting	repair records	transportation vehicles
maintenance	responsibilities	troubleshooting

What is an auto mechanic?

An auto mechanic works with a variety of (1) _____, such as automobiles, buses, and trucks. Auto mechanics do general repairs and (2) _____ on vehicles. Some mechanics (3) _____ engines, brakes, tires, or automobile technology or computers.

Auto mechanics have a variety of (4) _____. These include:

- Examining the vehicle and diagnosing a variety of issues

- Using power tools and (5) _____

- (6) _____ different vehicle systems

- Working with vehicle computers and (7) _____

- Performing routine maintenance

- (8) _____ and testing vehicles

- Updating maintenance and (9) _____

Auto mechanics work in various settings, such as (10) _____, garages, or car dealerships. Their responsibilities may differ based on where they work. For example, some (11) _____ may perform specialized tasks at a (12) _____, whereas mechanics who work in smaller repair shops may complete many different tasks.

A high school diploma or GED is the (13) _____ to become an auto mechanic. It's important for someone who wants to be a mechanic to have basic knowledge of (14) _____, reading, and writing. Some high schools also offer (15) _____ courses that students can take as electives.

F Listen and check your answers in **E**. 🎧

G Read the demographic information for mechanics. For each data set, create a graph using the visual given. Label each data point and give each graph a title.

```
100 |_____
 80 |
 60 |
 40 |
 20 |
  0 |_____
```
96% male
4% female

White: 65.6%
Hispanic or Latino: 17.2%
Black or African American: 9.9%
Asian: 4.6%
Unknown: 2.0%
American Indian and Alaska
Native: 0.7%

```
100 |_____
 75 |
 50 |
 25 |
  0 |_____
```
40+ years: 50%
30–40 years: 25%
20–30 years: 25%

H Write a short paragraph describing the demographics of mechanics in the United States.

_____

_____

_____

_____

I REFLECT Do you think a job as a mechanic would be a good choice for you? Why or why not?

_____

_____

_____

_____

Review

A **List four different types of cars.**

1. _____   2. _____

3. _____   4. _____

Which type of car is best for you? _____

B **Recall the auto maintenance tips you learned in Lesson 2. Write the correct verb from the box to complete each tip. You will need to use some of the verbs more than once.**

change	check	fill	inspect	perform	replace	top off

1. _____ a radiator flush.   2. _____ your air filter.

3. _____ an oil change.   4. _____ your brakes.

5. _____ your wipers.   6. _____ and

_____ your coolant.

7. _____ your oil levels.   8. _____ a timing belt

inspection.

9. _____ your washer fluid.   10. _____ your wheel

bolts.

11. _____ your power

steering fluid.

C **Calculate Gary's gas mileage and how much he is spending on gas. With a partner, discuss five ways Gary can improve his gas mileage.**

Date	Odometer	Trip	Gallons	MPG	Cost per Gallon	Cost per Mile
2/7	46,269	310 miles	15		$3.02	
2/17	46,579	325 miles	16		$2.90	
2/28	46,904	320 miles	15.5		$2.95	
3/5	47,224	280 miles	17		$3.01	

Learner Log	I can purchase a car. ☐ Yes ☐ No ☐ Maybe	I can maintain and repair a car. ☐ Yes ☐ No ☐ Maybe	I can compute mileage and gas consumption. ☐ Yes ☐ No ☐ Maybe

D Read the insurance policy and answer the questions on a separate piece of paper.

 DriveRite Automotive Insurance Co., Inc.

Dung Nguyen 79563 Eastern Way Ambrose, GA 31512	Policy Number: QPX2 80 56 45F5542 6 Policy Period: 2/10/22-8/10/23	Vehicle: 2019 Folks Passerine VIN: ZXYI493807T984XXX Annual Mileage: 12,500

Type of Coverage	Cost of Coverage	Limits of Liability
A. Medical	$182.50	Each person $100,000 Each accident $300,000
B. Liability	$175.00	Each person $100,000 Each accident $300,000
C. Collision	$98.26	Each person $50,000 Each accident $50,000
D. Uninsured motorist	$135.00	Each accident $150,000
E. Comprehensive	$76.45	Each incident $25,000

Premium: **$667.21**

1. Who is being insured through this insurance policy?

2. Where does the insured live?

3. How long is this policy in effect?

4. What is the total premium for the insured's policy?

5. How many miles does the insured drive per year?

6. The insured got in an accident last week, broke his leg, and damaged his car. Which types of coverage will pay for this?

7. How much is the insurance company charging for comprehensive coverage?

8. If the insured's car gets stolen, how much will the insurance company pay to replace the car?

9. What is the most the insurance company will pay for the property damage in an accident?

10. How much will the insurance company pay for each person who is hurt in an accident caused by someone without insurance?

E On a separate piece of paper, write a summary of one of these topics.

- Purchasing a car
- Keeping track of gas mileage
- Maintaining a car
- The benefits of driving an electric vehicle
- Saving money on gas
- Rules of the road

Vocabulary Review

A Write the name of each car part. What does each part do? With a partner, take turns describing each part and its function.

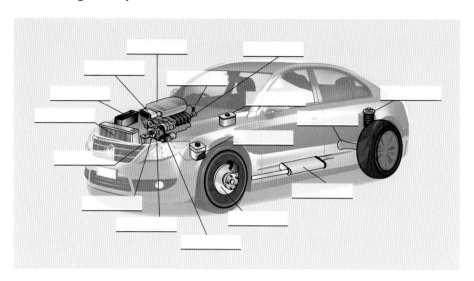

B Write a definition for each of the words. Use full sentences.

1. coverage: _Coverage is what the insurance company will pay for._ _____

2. premium: _____

3. collision: _____

4. mpg: _____

5. carpool: _____

6. kWh: _____

C Read each phrase and match it with a vocabulary word or phrase from the unit.

1. restrains driver and / or passengers in an accident: _____ _seat belt_ _____

2. identifies your vehicle: _____

3. covers damage to another vehicle: _____

4. can get clogged and affect your gas mileage: _____

5. tells you how fast you can drive on any given road: _____

6. the different things an insurance company will pay for: _____

7. tells you how many miles you have driven: _____

Team Project

Create an Auto Safety Handbook

SOFT SKILL ▶ Collaboration

With your class, you will compile an auto safety handbook.

1. Form a team of four or five students. Choose positions for each member of your team.

Position	Job Description	Student Name
Student 1: Project Leader	Check that everyone speaks English. Check that everyone participates.	
Student 2: Secretary	Take notes on team's ideas.	
Student 3: Designer	Design layout of handbook section.	
Student 4: Spokesperson	Prepare team for presentation.	
Student 5: Assistant	Help secretary and designer with their work.	

2. As a class, brainstorm a list of topics to include in your auto safety handbook. You might include safety maintenance tips, insurance minimums, and rules of the road. Count the number of teams and narrow your list of topics down to that number. Each team must choose a single topic to work on.

3. As a team, gather all the information for your group's section of the handbook.

4. Decide how you would like to present your information. You can choose pictures, lists of facts, and graphs. Be creative!

5. Create your section of the handbook.

6. Present your section of the handbook to the class.

7. Compile all the sections into one handbook.

COLLABORATION:
Negotiation
As you collaborate, practice negotiating by making polite suggestions:
I think it would be a great idea if we include…
Why don't we add…?
I think it would be better if…
I'm not sure that's such a good idea.
Wouldn't it be better if…?

Reading Challenge

A **PREDICT** Look at the title and read the quote. What job do you think Yu-Guo Guo has?

B Batteries allow us to use things without having to plug them in. Make a list of things that use batteries.

1. _____   2. _____

3. _____   4. _____

5. _____   6. _____

7. _____   8. _____

C Discuss the following questions in a small group.

1. Do you drive a car? Why?

2. Do you think cars are bad for the environment? Why?

D Yu-Guo Guo is a chemist who has been working with nanotechnology to change the way cars are made. Read the interview.

E Based on the interview, match each vocabulary expression to its correct meaning.

_____ 1. sustainable   a. rechargeable power source

_____ 2. lithium-ion battery b. microscopic particle of matter

_____ 3. deterioration   c. not wanted or wished for

_____ 4. nanoparticle   d. fuel formed from the remains of living organisms

_____ 5. fossil fuels   e. able to be maintained at a certain rate or level

_____ 6. undesirable   f. process of becoming progressively worse

F **INFER** Underline any words or phrases in the article that you don't understand and try to infer the meanings.

Fully Charged

Q: Why is there a need for electric vehicles (EVs)?

Yu-Guo Guo: There is a serious need for sustainable energy sources to power electrical devices, cars being one of them. Traditional sources, such as fossil fuels, cannot satisfy the growing demand, and the carbon emissions that cars give off raise great environmental concerns.

5 **Q: If that is the case, why don't more people drive EVs?**

Yu-Guo Guo: EVs are expensive because of the battery pack—the most important part of any EV. Batteries that are powerful enough to make cars go long distances are big and heavy, which makes an EV too costly for most consumers. On the other hand, using a smaller battery pack means the car couldn't go as far, making them undesirable for most drivers.

10 **Q: So, is there a feasible solution?**

Yu-Guo Guo: The key to improving performance and lowering the battery cost is using nanoparticles that can quickly absorb and hold many lithium ions. This will improve the performance without causing deterioration in the electrode. In plain terms, this means that cars won't drain the energy storage capacity quickly. Compared with traditional lithium-ion

15 batteries, this new high-power technology means batteries can be fully charged in just a few minutes, as quickly and easily as you fill your car with gas. These advanced batteries recover more energy when cars stop, deliver more power when cars start, and enable vehicles to run longer.

Q: Why hasn't this been done before?

20 **Yu-Guo Guo:** I invented the technology, so it hasn't been possible before. I found a unique way to make an important part of this technology—lithium iron phosphate—less expensive and easier for manufacturers to work with.

Q: How soon will we start to see EVs with the better, smaller battery packs?

Yu-Guo Guo: Production of smaller, lighter battery packs will begin in 2023.

"There is a serious need for sustainable energy sources to power electrical devices."
—Yu-Guo Guo

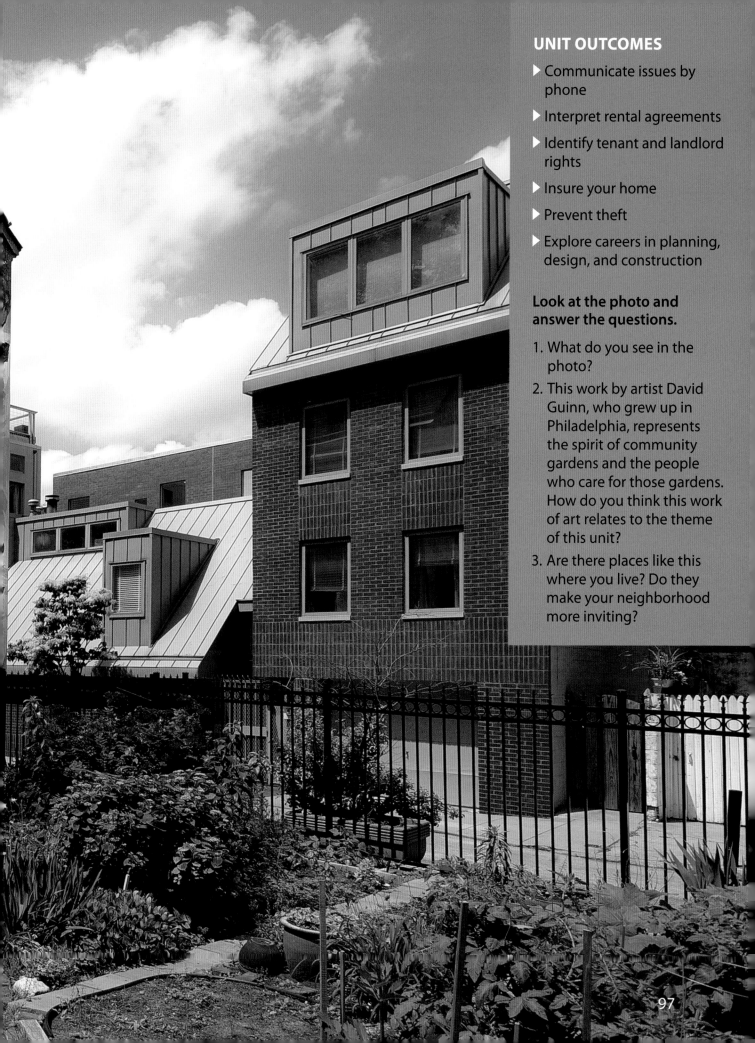

UNIT OUTCOMES

▶ Communicate issues by phone

▶ Interpret rental agreements

▶ Identify tenant and landlord rights

▶ Insure your home

▶ Prevent theft

▶ Explore careers in planning, design, and construction

Look at the photo and answer the questions.

1. What do you see in the photo?

2. This work by artist David Guinn, who grew up in Philadelphia, represents the spirit of community gardens and the people who care for those gardens. How do you think this work of art relates to the theme of this unit?

3. Are there places like this where you live? Do they make your neighborhood more inviting?

Vocabulary Builder

A **What do the following words have in common? Write the theme.**

abandon	dwelling	grounds	summon
burglarize	enticing	premises	theft
crime	evident	responsible	thief
disturbance	exterior	seize	weapons

Theme: _____

B **CLASSIFY Put each word in A in the correct column according to its part of speech. Use a dictionary if you need help.**

Noun	Verb	Adjective

C **Choose two words from each column in B. Write one sentence using each word.**

1. _____
2. _____
3. _____
4. _____
5. _____
6. _____

D Read. 🎧

You can often identify a word's part of speech just by looking at it. The following words are nouns. What do they have in common?

prevention   installation   expiration

The roots of these words are verbs: *prevent, install,* and *expire.* The suffix *-(a)tion* changes each verb into a noun. The noun form indicates an action or process of doing an action. For example, *prevention* signifies the action of preventing something.

E **Change each verb into its noun form. Then define each new word on a separate piece of paper. Use a dictionary to check your spelling.**

1. activate _____

2. compensate _____

3. deteriorate _____

4. estimate _____

5. litigate _____

6. possess _____

7. terminate _____

8. vacate _____

F **Without using a dictionary, match the phrases with their definitions.**

_____ 1. fit for human occupancy   a. advance warning written in a business letter

_____ 2. formal written notice   b. estimate of how much one might pay for a policy

_____ 3. full compliance   c. being gone for a long time; longer than expected

_____ 4. housing codes   d. built well; building in good condition

_____ 5. insurance quote   e. doing what one is required to do

_____ 6. prolonged absence   f. government regulations for building houses

_____ 7. replacement cost   g. government rules regarding health and cleanliness

_____ 8. sanitary regulations   h. suitable for people to live in

_____ 9. structurally sound   i. taking up a lot of time

_____ 10. time-consuming   j. price you have to pay to change something that is broken for something new

I Have a Problem

GOAL ▶ Communicate issues by phone

A Read these lines of a text chain between Ming and her landlord. 🎧

Ming: Mr. Martin, this is Ming Mei your tenant from Spring Street. Our roof is leaking. Can you please send someone to fix it?

Mr. Martin: Hi, Ming. Can you please call me? I have a few questions.

B Read and listen to the phone conversation Ming Mei has with her landlord. 🎧

Landlord: Hello?

Ming Mei: Hi, Mr. Martin. This is Ming Mei from the apartment on Spring Street.

Landlord: Oh, hi, Ming Mei. What's going on with the roof?

Ming Mei: Well, after all the rain we had this weekend, the roof started leaking. I think there may be a pool of water still on the roof because water is leaking through our ceiling even though the rain stopped.

Landlord: Oh, no. Has it damaged the carpet?

Ming Mei: No, we caught it right away and put a bucket down to collect the drips.

Landlord: Oh, great. Thanks for being on top of it. I'll have my handyman come over and look at the roof and your ceiling. Can you let him in around ten this morning?

Ming Mei: I have to go to work, but I can get my sister to come over.

Landlord: Great. Thanks for calling, Ming Mei.

Ming Mei: Thank you, Mr. Martin.

C Practice the conversation in **B** with a partner. Then switch roles.

D Listen to the conversations between tenants and landlords. Take notes in the table. 🎧

	Problem	Solution
Conversation 1		
Conversation 2		
Conversation 3		

E Look at the following statements from the conversation between Ming Mei and her landlord in **B**. Answer the questions.

I'll have my handyman come over and look at the roof and your ceiling.

1. Who is the subject of the sentence? _____

2. Who is going to come over? _____

… I can get my sister to come over.

3. Who is the subject of the sentence? _____

4. Who is going to come over? _____

F Study the chart with your teacher.

Causative Verbs: *Get, Have, Help, Let, Make*			
Subject	**Verb**	**Noun / Pronoun**	**Infinitive (Omit *to* except with *get*.)**
He	will get	his handyman	to come.
She	had	her mom	wait for the repairperson.
The landlord	helped	me	move in.
Mr. Martin	let	Ming Mei	skip one month's rent.
Ming Mei	makes	her sister	pay half of the rent.
Use: We use causative verb structures to indicate that the subject causes something to happen.			

G Match each causative verb from **F** with its meaning. Two verbs have the same meaning.

_____ 1. get   a. allow

_____ 2. have   b. provide assistance

_____ 3. help   c. delegate responsibility to someone

_____ 4. let   d. require

_____ 5. make

H Unscramble the words and phrases to make causative statements. Then write housing-related sentences of your own using the same verbs.

1. them / had / their landlord / leave a deposit

   Their landlord had them leave a deposit.

   My wife had me paint the children's bedroom.

2. to prospective renters / him / let / the apartment / show / Mario's tenants

   _____

   _____

3. pay / made / my parents / for rent / me

   _____

   _____

4. my boss / for me / will get / I / to write / a letter of reference

   _____

   _____

5. her husband / she / which house to rent / decide / will let

   _____

   _____

6. find / my cousin / me / a new place to live / helped

   _____

   _____

I SEQUENCE What should you do when you call your landlord? Read the sentences and put them in the correct order (1–4).

_____ Restate the solution for clarification.   _____ Ask for a solution.

_____ Clearly identify the problem.   _____ State your name and where you live.

J What are some problems you might have with your home that would require you to call your landlord? Brainstorm a list with a partner on a separate piece of paper.

K With your partner, practice conversations with a landlord about the problems you brainstormed in J. Follow the order of events from I.

Understand the Fine Print

GOAL ▶ Interpret rental agreements

A Have you ever rented a property? If so, do you remember the information that was in your rental agreement? Make a list on a separate piece of paper.

B Rental agreements are long and contain information to protect the tenant and the landlord. Read the financial section from a rental agreement from California.

RENT: To pay as rental the sum of $ _____ per month, due and payable in advance from the first day of every month. Failure to pay rent when due will result in the Owner taking immediate legal action to evict the Resident from the premises and seize the security deposit.

LATE FEE: Rent received after the first of the month will be subject to a late fee of 10% monthly rent.

SECURITY DEPOSIT: Resident agrees to pay a deposit in the amount of $ _____ to secure Resident's pledge of full compliance with the terms of this agreement. The security deposit will be used at the end of the tenancy to compensate the Owner for any damages or unpaid rent or charges. Further damages will be repaired at Resident's expense with funds other than the deposit.

RETURN OF DEPOSIT: Security deposits will be deposited for the Resident's benefit in a non-interest-bearing bank account. Release of these deposits is subject to the provisions of State Statutes and as follows:

A. The full term of this agreement has been completed.

B. Formal written notice has been given.

C. No damage or deterioration to the premises, building(s), or grounds is evident.

D. The entire dwelling, appliances, closets, and cupboards are clean and left free of insects; the refrigerator is defrosted; all debris and garbage has been removed from the property; the carpets are cleaned and left odorless.

E. Any and all unpaid charges, pet charges, late charges, extra visitor charges, delinquent rents, utility charges, etc., have been paid in full.

F. All keys have been returned, including keys to any new locks installed while Resident was in possession.

G. A forwarding address has been left with the Owner.

Thirty days after termination of occupancy, the Owner will send the balance of the deposit to the address provided by the Resident, payable to the signatories hereto, or the Owner will impose a claim on the deposit and so notify the Resident by certified letter. If such written claim is not sent, the Owner relinquishes the right to make any further claim on the deposit and must return it to the Resident provided Resident has given the Owner notice of intent to vacate, abandon, and terminate this agreement prior to the expiration of its full term, at least 7 days in advance.

C In a group, interpret the financial section of the rental agreement. Underline words or phrases no one in your group understands and ask your teacher.

D Read the sections on maintenance and repairs from a rental agreement from California. 🎧

MAINTENANCE: Resident agrees to maintain the premises during the period of this agreement. This includes woodwork, floors, walls, furnishings and fixtures, appliances, windows, screen doors, lawns, landscaping, fences, plumbing, electrical, air-conditioning and heating, and mechanical systems. Tacks, nails, or other hangers nailed or screwed into the walls or ceilings will be removed at the termination of this agreement. Damage caused by rain, hail, or wind as a result of leaving windows or doors open, or damage caused by overflow of water, or stoppage of waste pipes, breakage of glass, damage to screens, deterioration of lawns and landscaping—whether caused by abuse or neglect—is the responsibility of the Resident.

RESIDENT'S OBLIGATIONS: The Resident agrees to meet all Resident's obligations including:

A. Taking affirmative action to ensure that nothing exists that might place the Owner in violation of applicable building, housing, and health codes.

B. Keeping the dwelling clean and sanitary; removing garbage and trash as they accumulate; maintaining plumbing in good working order to prevent stoppages and / or leakage of plumbing, fixtures, faucets, pipes, etc.

C. Operating all electrical, plumbing, sanitary, heating, ventilating, a/c, and other appliances in a reasonable and safe manner.

D. Assuring that property belonging to the Owner is safeguarded against damage, destruction, loss, removal, or theft.

REPAIRS: In the event repairs are needed beyond the competence of the Resident, he or she is urged to arrange for professional assistance. Residents are offered the discount as an incentive to make their own decisions on the property they live in. Therefore, as much as possible, the Resident should refrain from contacting the Owner except for emergencies or for repairs costing more than the discount since such involvement by the Owner will result in the loss of the discount. ANY REPAIR THAT WILL COST MORE THAN THE AMOUNT OF THE DISCOUNT MUST BE APPROVED BY THE OWNER OR THE TENANT WILL BE RESPONSIBLE FOR THE ENTIRE COST OF THAT REPAIR. Any improvement made by the tenant shall become the property of the Owner at the conclusion of this agreement.

E Divide into two groups. Prepare and give a presentation. One group will present the responsibilities for maintenance, and the other group will present the responsibilities for repairs.

F SUMMARIZE Make a summary of your section for the class.

G Based on what you have read so far, what do you think the rental agreement will say about each of the following items? Write your ideas.

Lead-based paint: _____

Wear and tear vs. damage: _____

Smoke detectors: _____

Utilities: _____

H Read the information taken from the rental agreement about the topics in **G**. Write the correct topic on the line that follows each section.

1. The cost of repairing or replacing items damaged beyond wear and tear will be paid by the Owner / Landlord unless the Resident willfully or through lack of due care caused or permitted the damage.

   _____

2. Smoke and carbon monoxide detectors have been installed in this residence. It's the Resident's responsibility to maintain appliances including testing periodically and replacing batteries as recommended by the manufacturer. In the event the detectors are missing or inoperative, the tenant has an affirmative duty to notify the landlord immediately.

   _____

3. Resident shall be responsible for payments of the following utilities: electricity, water, gas. The landlord pays for garbage pickup. He / She specifically authorizes the Owner to deduct amounts of unpaid bills from their deposits in the event they remain unpaid after the termination of this agreement.

   _____

4. Houses built before 1978 may contain lead-based paint. Lead from paint, paint chips, and dust can pose health hazards if not taken care of properly. Lead exposure is especially harmful to young children and pregnant women. Before renting pre-1978 housing, Owner must disclose the presence of known lead-based paint and lead-based paint hazards in the dwelling. Resident must also receive a federally approved pamphlet of lead-poisoning prevention.

   _____

I SUMMARIZE With a partner, go back through the sections of the rental agreement in this lesson. Make a list of all the topics. Then, on a separate piece of paper, write a statement about each topic, summarizing what the rental agreement says about it.

Your Rights

GOAL ▶ Identify tenant and landlord rights

A **Discuss the following terms with a partner. Define them with your teacher.**

1. What is a *right*?

_____

2. What is a *responsibility*?

_____

B **Tenants have rights and responsibilities, just as landlords do. Read the list and indicate which responsibility belongs to each person: tenant (*T*) or landlord (*L*).**

1. _____ Provide a clean apartment when the tenant moves in.

2. _____ Maintain common areas (hallways, stairs, yards, entryways).

3. _____ Give the landlord permission to enter the apartment at reasonable times and with advance notice to inspect it or to make any necessary repairs.

4. _____ Keep noise at a level that will not disturb neighbors.

5. _____ Keep the apartment and the surrounding area clean and in good condition.

6. _____ Notify the landlord immediately if the apartment needs repair through no fault of the tenant.

7. _____ Notify the landlord of any anticipated prolonged absence from the apartment so he or she can keep an eye on things.

8. _____ Pay the rent on time.

9. _____ Provide properly working plumbing and heating (both hot and cold running water).

10. _____ Repair any damage occurring to the apartment through the fault of the tenant, tenant's family members, or tenant's guests. Notify landlord at once of major damage.

11. _____ Provide well-lit hallways and entryways.

12. _____ When moving out, give landlord proper advance notice. Be sure that the apartment is in the same condition as when the tenant moved in and return the key to the landlord promptly.

C **RESTATE** **With a partner, restate each of the responsibilities in B.**

EXAMPLE: It is a landlord's responsibility to provide a clean apartment when the tenant moves in.

D Read about the implied warranty of habitability.

The *implied warranty of habitability* states that a landlord must keep the property in a condition fit for human occupancy. In other words, it must be a safe place for human beings to live. Here are some questions a landlord might ask him- or herself before renting a property: Are there any known hazards with the property? Do the fixtures work properly? Is the building structurally sound? Does the property have any recurring problems?

If a landlord does not comply with the implied warranty of habitability, a tenant can cancel the lease, leave the premises, take the costs of repairs out of the rent, or ask for monetary damages.

In determining whether a landlord has violated the implied warranty of habitability, courts will look at several factors:

1. Is the problem violating a housing code?
2. Is the problem violating a sanitary regulation?
3. Is the problem affecting a needed facility?
4. How long has the problem lasted?
5. How old is the building?
6. How much is the rent?
7. Has the tenant been ignoring the problem?
8. Is the tenant in any way responsible for the problem?

One or more of these factors will help the courts determine who is at fault and what the victim's rights may be.

E ANALYZE In a small group, discuss the following questions.

1. If your landlord violated the implied warranty of habitability, what could you do?

_____

_____

2. According to the list of questions that courts will ask, what are some situations in which you could take a landlord to court?

_____

_____

3. What are some situations when you couldn't take a landlord to court?

_____

_____

F With a partner, look at each photo. Decide if it violates the implied warranty of habitability. Imagine that each of these situations has gone on for at least three weeks with no response from the landlord.

G Imagine that you are a landlord. Use the responsibilities in **B** to write statements using causative verb structures.

1. *The law makes me provide a clean apartment for the tenant when he or she moves in.*

2. _____

3. _____

4. _____

5. _____

H Imagine that you are a tenant. Use the responsibilities in **B** to write statements using causative verb structures.

1. *The law makes me pay the rent on time.*

2. _____

3. _____

4. _____

5. _____

Insuring Your Home

GOAL ▶ Insure your home

A CONTRAST Discuss.

1. Do you have insurance for your property? Why or why not?

2. What is the difference between homeowner's insurance and renter's insurance? What do you think each covers?

B Discuss the terms of this renter's insurance quote.

Renter's Insurance Quote	
Value of Personal Property	$20,000
Liability	$100,000
Medical Payments	$1,000
Loss of Use	$4,000
Loss of Rental Income	$10,000
Monthly Payment	$13.92
Deductible	$1000

C Listen to Makela and Bryce discuss the renter's insurance quote. Then match the insurance coverage with its definition.

_____ 1. medical payments

_____ 2. liability

_____ 3. loss of use

_____ 4. personal property

_____ 5. deductible

_____ 6. loss of rental income

a. pays for you to rent another house or hotel room if you can't live in your home for some reason, like fire or water damage

b. helps pay medical expenses if someone has an accident or is injured while at your home, whether or not you're responsible

c. the amount you have to pay before the insurance company will pay

d. pays for your personal belongings if they are stolen or damaged while in the home

e. covers the landlord if the property is uninhabitable due to a fire, smoke, explosion, or water damage caused by you

f. protects against lawsuits due to accidents in your property, and pays for the cost of hiring a lawyer to defend you

D **CALCULATE** What is the value of your personal property? On a separate piece of paper, list each of these items and write next to it what it would cost to replace them: appliances, computers, tablets, dishes / cookware, fitness / sport equipment, furniture, jewelry / watches, silverware / linens, tools. Add any other valuables you may have that are not on the list.

EXAMPLE: _tools: $2,000_ _____

E Read the Lugos' homeowner's insurance policy. Then answer the questions.

State One Insurance	
Name and Address of Insured: Rafael and Elba Lugo 7930 Inca Way Kansas City, MO 64108	
Deductible: $2,500	**Annual Premium: $1,077.93**
Coverage Type	**Amount of Coverage**
Dwelling	$401,000
Personal Property	$300,750
Loss of Use	$80,200
Personal Liability—Each Occurrence	$100,000
Medical Payments to Others—Each Person	$1,000

1. How much will the insurance company pay to rebuild the house? _____

2. How much will the insurance company pay to replace personal belongings? _____

3. How much will the family have to pay before the insurance company pays? _____

4. What is the monthly premium? _____

Homeowners are responsible for their own maintenance costs.

F Read about the Lugos' home. Then fill in the information about your home or a place where you have lived before.

Building Feature	Lugos' Home	My Home
Year built	1986	
Total square footage	2,378 sq. ft.	
Number of stories	2	
Exterior wall construction material	stucco on frame	
Roof type	clay tile	
Garage or carport	attached garage: 2-car	
Wall partitions construction materials	drywall	
Wall / Floor covering materials	paint / wood and tile	
Number of kitchens / bathrooms	1 / 3	
Type of air / heat	central air / gas	

G On a separate piece of paper, answer the questions that apply to you. If you prefer to not share personal information, use imaginary details.

I have insurance.

1. Policy type: homeowner's or renter's?

2. How long have you had your policy?

3. What is your monthly premium?

4. How often do you review your policy?

I don't have insurance.

1. Policy you need: homeowner's or renter's?

2. How can you find an insurance company?

3. How much personal property coverage do you need?

4. How much can you spend per month on insurance? ($50, $100, $150)

H Using the questions in **G**, interview three classmates. Write their answers in your notebook.

I On a separate piece of paper, write a statement about what you are going to do to protect your home and personal property.

EXAMPLE: *I need renter's insurance for my personal property. This week, I'm going to go online and get quotes from three insurance companies.*

Protecting Your Home

GOAL ▶ Prevent theft

A Listen to the statistics on burglaries in the United States and fill in the missing numbers and words. 🎧

Did you know . . . ?

- There are over (1) _____ burglaries per year in the United States.

- (2) _____ of homeowners don't have a security system.

- (3) _____ has the most property crimes.

- Over (4) _____ of homes will get broken into in the next 20 years.

- (5) _____ of home burglaries are repeated within 6 weeks.

- (6) _____ of people who have been burglarized know the burglar.

B Discuss these statistics with your partner. Are you surprised? Why do you think some of these are true?

C Use a dictionary to define the words. Include the part of speech for each word. Then answer the questions.

burglar: _____

burglarize / burgle: _____

burglary: _____

theft: _____

thief: _____

thieve: _____

1. What is the difference between the two sets of words? _____

_____

2. There are three pairs of synonyms in the sets of words. Write them on a separate piece of paper.

D PREDICT You are about to read a newsletter on how to protect your home from being burglarized. What do you think it will say about the following items? Brainstorm with a group.

Light	Time	Noise

E Read the newsletter.

Theft Prevention Newsletter

Burglary Prevention

Each year in the US, there are more than 1 million home burglaries. Nine out of ten of these crimes are preventable. The risk of being burglarized can be greatly reduced by taking simple steps to make your home more difficult to enter and less enticing to would-be burglars. **Remember the greatest weapons in the fight to prevent burglaries are light, time, and noise.**

Light

- ○ Mount exterior lights out of reach so burglars can't unscrew bulbs.
- ○ Consider buying motion-sensitive lights, which are now relatively cheap.
- ○ Use a variable light timer to activate lights inside your home.
- ○ Trim trees and shrubs near doors and windows so burglars can't hide in the shadows.

Time

Make it time-consuming for a burglar to break into your home:

- ○ Install deadbolt locks on all exterior doors.
- ○ Install double key locks in doors that contain glass. This keeps burglars from being able to open the door simply by breaking the glass and reaching through.
  (Note: So that everyone in the house can get out in the event of a fire, keep the key in a designated place.)
- ○ Place additional locks on all windows and patio doors.

Noise

- ○ Get a dog. You don't need a large attack dog; even a small dog creates a disturbance that burglars would prefer to avoid. Remember to license and vaccinate it.
- ○ Consider having someone care for your dogs in your home while you're away instead of boarding them.
- ○ If you can afford it, install an alarm system that will alert neighbors of a burglar's presence. Most systems can even summon local police directly.

Life ONLINE

Today, there are ways to monitor the outside of your home even if you are away. You can install cameras and even doorbell cameras that connect to your phone so you can see who is outside your home and communicate with them. Do you have any doorbells or cameras like these at your home?

F COMPARE Look at the ideas you brainstormed in **D** and the tips from the newsletter in **E**. Are there any tips you didn't think of? List them in the table.

Light	Time	Noise

G Listen to the police officer talk about other tips to prevent a break in. Write the tips. 🎧

1. _____

2. _____

3. _____

4. _____

5. _____

6. _____

H Sometimes all your efforts will not stop a determined burglar. It is wise to take some precautions that will help you get your property back should a criminal successfully break into your home. Listen to the police officer and take notes in your notebook. 🎧

I CREATE Make a flier to post in your community. Include the most important tips you learned about home theft prevention.

Some communities form Neighborhood Watch groups to look out for each other.

NEIGHBORHOOD WATCH

PROGRAM IN FORCE

We report all Suspicious Persons & Activities to our Law Enforcement Agency

LESSON
6

Explore the Workforce

GOAL ▶ Explore careers in planning, design, and construction

A **PREDICT** Look at the list of careers. What do you think each person does? Match the careers to the job descriptions.

Career	Job Description
_____ 1. architects	a. make precise measurements to determine property boundaries
_____ 2. architectural / engineering managers	b. collect data and make maps of the earth's surface
_____ 3. civil engineers	c. convert the designs of engineers and architects into technical drawings using software
_____ 4. construction / building inspectors	d. design parks and other outdoor spaces
_____ 5. construction managers	e. design, build, and supervise infrastructure* projects and systems
_____ 6. drafters	f. develop land use plans and programs that help create communities, accommodate population growth, and update physical facilities
_____ 7. landscape architects	g. ensure that construction meets building codes and ordinances, zoning regulations, and contract specifications
_____ 8. surveying / mapping technicians	h. plan and design houses, factories, office buildings, and other structures
_____ 9. surveyors	i. plan, coordinate, budget, and supervise construction projects from start to finish
_____ 10. urban / regional planners	j. plan, direct, and coordinate activities for architectural and engineering companies

*infrastructure: structures and facilities (buildings, roads, power, etc.) needed for a community to operate

B With a partner, practice talking about the careers in **A**.

Student A: What does an architect do?
Student B: An architect plans and designs houses, factories, office buildings, and other structures.

C Look at the list. Which careers do you think pay the most? The least? Discuss.

Surveying and Mapping Technicians _____

Drafters _____

Surveyors _____

Construction and Building Inspectors _____

Landscape Architects _____

Urban and Regional Planners _____

Architect _____

Civil Engineers _____

Construction Managers _____

Architectural and Engineering Managers _____

D These salaries are the 2021 median income for the careers above. Number the salaries in the correct order (1-10), from the lowest pay to the highest pay.

_____ $46,910   _____ $61,640

_____ $152,350   _____ $61,600

_____ $88,050   _____ $78,500

_____ $67,950   _____ $98,890

_____ $60,290   _____ $81,800

E Write the salaries from **D** on the lines in **C**. The jobs are listed in order from the lowest paid to the highest paid.

F Listen to the conversation about education required for the careers in **C**. Then write the careers under each column. 🎧

High School Diploma	Associate Degree	Bachelor's Degree	Master's Degree

G **COMPARE** Compare the degree required for each career with the salary. Do you think they match? Why or why not? Discuss with a small group and share your ideas with the class.

H Read the job ad and answer the questions.

Commercial Construction Project Manager

Posted 5 days ago   Full-time

This job is with a premier general contractor with a great reputation amongst its clients and employees. We are seeking a Commercial Construction Project Manager in the greater Houston area.

Minimum Qualifications Required:
- 5 years of commercial construction project management with a commercial general contractor
- experience managing a variety of projects in different phases of the construction process
- Bachelor's degree in Construction Management, Engineering, Architecture, or related field (preferred, but experience may be considered in lieu of those qualifications)
- urgency and resourcefulness in identifying and resolving problems
- flexibility to manage multiple tasks and projects simultaneously

For consideration please email your resume to tbrown@cmj.job.

1. Is this job full-time or part-time? _____

2. What degree is required? _____

3. How much experience is required? _____

4. What does *experience may be considered in lieu of those qualifications* mean?

   _____

   _____

   _____

5. **REFLECT** If you had the experience and education required, do you think you would be good at this job? Why or why not?

   _____

   _____

   _____

   _____

Review

A With a partner, practice conversations between a tenant and a landlord. Practice both face-to-face and phone conversations. Use these scenarios.

1. leaky faucet
2. broken window
3. can't pay rent on time
4. noisy neighbors

B Write complete sentences using the causative verb structure and the words provided. You may choose the verb form to use.

1. she / make / her sister / move

   She made her sister move out of her apartment.

2. I / get / her / meet

3. they / have / their friends / wait

4. Irina / help / her father / repair

5. my father / make / me / pay

6. his landlord / let / him / fix

C Make a list of topics that can be found in a rental agreement. After each topic, write a typical statement that might be found in such an agreement.

1. Rent: The rent must be paid on the first day of each month.

2.

3.

4.

5.

6.

Learner Log   I can communicate issues by phone.   I can interpret rental agreements.
    ☐ Yes ☐ No ☐ Maybe   ☐ Yes ☐ No ☐ Maybe

D **Write one right for tenants and one right for landlords.**

1. A tenant has the right to _____.

2. A landlord has the right to _____.

E **Read the insurance policy and answer the questions.**

Insurance Policy

Deductible: $2,250.00	Annual Premium: $989.45
Coverage Type	**Amount of Coverage**
Dwelling	$330,000
Loss of Use	$80,200
Medical Payments to Others—Each Person	$1,000
Personal Liability—Each Occurrence	$100,000
Personal Property	$200,000

1. Is this a homeowner's or renter's policy? _____

   How do you know? _____

2. How much will the insurance company pay to rebuild the house? _____

3. What is the annual premium? _____

4. How much will the insurance company pay to replace personal belongings? _____

F **Write _T_ for true or _F_ for false in front of each theft prevention tip.**

_____ 1. Place your valuables in easy-to-see locations.

_____ 2. Lock up anything that could be used to break into your home.

_____ 3. Install an alarm system.

_____ 4. Make sure you turn off all the lights when you leave your home.

_____ 5. Let your neighbors know when you will be out of town.

_____ 6. Install double key locks on all your windows.

Learner Log	I can identify tenant and landlord rights. Yes　No　Maybe	I can insure my home. Yes　No　Maybe	I can prevent theft. Yes　No　Maybe

Vocabulary Review

A Complete each question with a word or phrase from this unit. There may be more than one correct answer.

1. Are you a tenant or a _____?

2. How much _____ do you have for your personal property?

3. Do you have _____ or _____ insurance?

4. What is your monthly _____?

5. Do you have an _____ installed in your house?

6. What would your landlord do if there were a _____ in your building?

B With a partner, ask and answer the questions in **A**.

C Without using a dictionary, define these words. Include the part of speech.

1. dwelling: _____

2. policy: _____

3. right: _____

4. burglary: _____

5. responsibility: _____

6. prevent: _____

7. vacate: _____

8. premium: _____

D With a partner, write a conversation using as many of the words from **C** as you can.

Student A: _____

Student B: _____

Student A: _____

Student B: _____

Student A: _____

Student B: _____

Student A: _____

Student B: _____

Housing Presentation

SOFT SKILL ▶ Presentation Skills

Presentation Topics
- Communication with a landlord or tenant
- Rental agreements
- Tenant and landlord rights
- Renter's or homeowner's insurance
- Theft prevention

1. Form a team of four or five students. Decide which topic your team will work on. (Each team should choose a different topic from the list above.)

2. Choose positions for each member of your team.

Position	Job Description	Student Name
Student 1: Project Leader	Check that everyone speaks English. Check that everyone participates.	
Student 2: Project Secretary	Take notes on your team's ideas.	
Student 3: Coordinator	Divide presentation into parts. Assign each team member one part of the presentation.	
Student 4: Director	Organize a different method of presentation for each part.	
Student 5: Advisor	Give feedback on the presentation as each team member rehearses their part.	

3. Gather the information for your presentation.

4. Decide how to present your information to the class. For example, you may want to use charts, role plays, or games.

5. Create any materials needed for your presentation.

6. Rehearse your presentation.

7. Give your presentation to the class.

PRESENTATION SKILLS

Memorize

1. If you have time, memorize your part of the presentation. You can still refer to your notes but it will go more smoothly if you have it memorized.

Show

2. Using slides, charts, or pictures to illustrate what you are presenting is a great way to keep your audience engaged but will also help you remember the information you are presenting.

Ask

3. Asking your audience questions during your presentation is another great way to hold their attention. It will also also take the focus off of you for a bit.

Reading Challenge

A **Work through these steps with a partner.**

1. Do you know what *prefab* means?

2. Sometimes you have to break up a word to understand its meaning. Look at the two parts. Now do you know what it means?

   pre   fabricated

3. *Prefab* is most often used to refer to the construction of buildings. What do you think a *prefab building* is?

B **Read** *The Prefab Home: More Sustainable?*

C **Choose the best answer.**

1. What is NOT one of the four things that make prefab homes sustainable?

   a. recycled materials used

   b. no wasted building materials

   c. durable

   d. less expensive

2. What does *structurally sound* mean in line 22?

   a. The walls are very thick so the sound doesn't travel to other parts of the house.

   b. The house is built very well and it won't fall apart.

   c. The structure was made with a sounding board.

   d. Prefab homes are built without making any noise.

D **COMPARE With a partner, complete the Venn diagram comparing a prefab home to a conventionally built home.**

Prefab   Conventional

The Prefab Home: More Sustainable? 🎧

Have you ever thought of buying a prefab home? The average cost of a new home built in the US in 2021 was $288,000. What if you could buy that same house for $180,000? A
5 prefab home is built in a factory and shipped in pieces for workers to assemble on site or sometimes it is built completely at a factory and then delivered in one piece. Not only are prefab homes less expensive, but they are good
10 for the environment. The house in the photo, for example, has a solar water heating system, an irrigation system that uses water from the washing machine, the shower and the sinks, and uses recycled materials and wood from responsibly managed forests.

Prefab, modular green designed by architect Ray Kappe, Santa Monica, California

15 LESS WASTE

There is a formula for prefab homes. They are prebuilt according to very specific measurements so there should be no excess building materials. Manufacturers know ahead of time exactly how much of each material is required. And since these materials are stored in a factory instead of a construction site, there is less of a chance of them being stolen or damaged.

20 DURABLE

Prefab homes are more durable than traditionally built homes. Since they often have to be shipped (driven) a long way, they are built to be more structurally sound. The house frame is reinforced for delivery which means they are built of very sturdy materials. In other words, the house will last longer.

25 ECO-FRIENDLY

There is more of a focus on clean and green energy in prefab homes; therefore, they are built using non-toxic materials. They are also built with the environment in mind by using recycled materials for internal walls, insulation, and roofs. In addition, the greenhouse gas-related impact of these modular homes is 53% less than conventional structures. Building a conventional home
30 releases double the amount of carbon dioxide.

ENERGY and WATER EFFICIENT

Modular homes are built as more tightly sealed structures, meaning they waste less energy. This could lower heating and cooling costs. Also, prefab homes are built using sustainable sources of energy, such as solar panels, which makes them a much more energy-efficient solution. They
35 also use low-energy lighting, like LEDs. Similarly, prefab homes are water efficient, reducing freshwater consumption to up to 40% less than conventional homes.

Although it may be tricky to find a piece of land to put your prefab home on, the cost and sustainability may make it worth it. And prefab homes typically only take about three months to build, which is about how long it would take to prepare the land for a conventional home to be
40 built. Something to think about!

Keeping It Professional

What do you think this man is reacting to? Have you had reactions like this one when checking social media?

Before You Watch

A Choose the tools you use in a professional setting (at work or school). Then share your answers with a partner.

☐ email ☐ texts ☐ social media ☐ video calling

B Read the words and expressions. Then write them next to the correct definitions.

best practices	case-by-case	cross the line	reply all	takeaways	time-sensitive

1. _____: key ideas or conclusions from a presentation

2. _____: actions that experts agree will lead to good results

3. _____: an email option in which you respond to everyone who received the original message

4. _____: one at a time; considering each situation individually

5. _____: to do or say something inappropriate or offensive

6. _____: urgent or requiring a quick response

C This video gives tips for communicating in a professional setting. What best practices do you follow? What do you think the video will mention?

D Watch the video. Choose the topics discussed.

☐ 1. using email vs. texting

☐ 2. different rules for friends and coworkers

☐ 3. timing of emails

☐ 4. email signatures

☐ 5. time-sensitive issues vs. routine questions

☐ 6. appropriate greetings

☐ 7. sharing personal information

☐ 8. length of phone calls

☐ 9. using emojis

☐ 10. individual communication styles

E Read the statements and watch the video again. Who expresses each opinion or preference: Alex, April, or Mike?

1. I don't want to get messages from students during my time off. _____Mike_____

2. I only reply to emails during working hours. _____ and _____

3. Texts are appropriate for time-sensitive issues. _____

4. Texting or email can be appropriate depending on the relationship. _____

After You Watch

F Match the speaker's statements to the related communication advice.

_____ 1. **Alex:** A student texted me with personal questions that are not relevant to school.

_____ 2. **Alex:** My boss emails me at midnight and wants an immediate response.

_____ 3. **April:** A student friended me on social media after our first class.

_____ 4. **Alex:** I spilled coffee on myself and told the whole school about it.

a. Avoid connecting with someone on social media if you've only met in a professional setting.

b. It's important to respect people's personal time.

c. Be careful when using *reply all*.

d. Personal questions aren't appropriate in professional communication.

G What is your communication style? Discuss the questions with a partner. Do you agree on what's appropriate and what's not?

1. When is it appropriate to use email, texting or messaging apps, and social media?

2. How are your communication preferences different in personal and professional contexts?

3. What can others do to show that they respect your time and your personal life?

5 Health

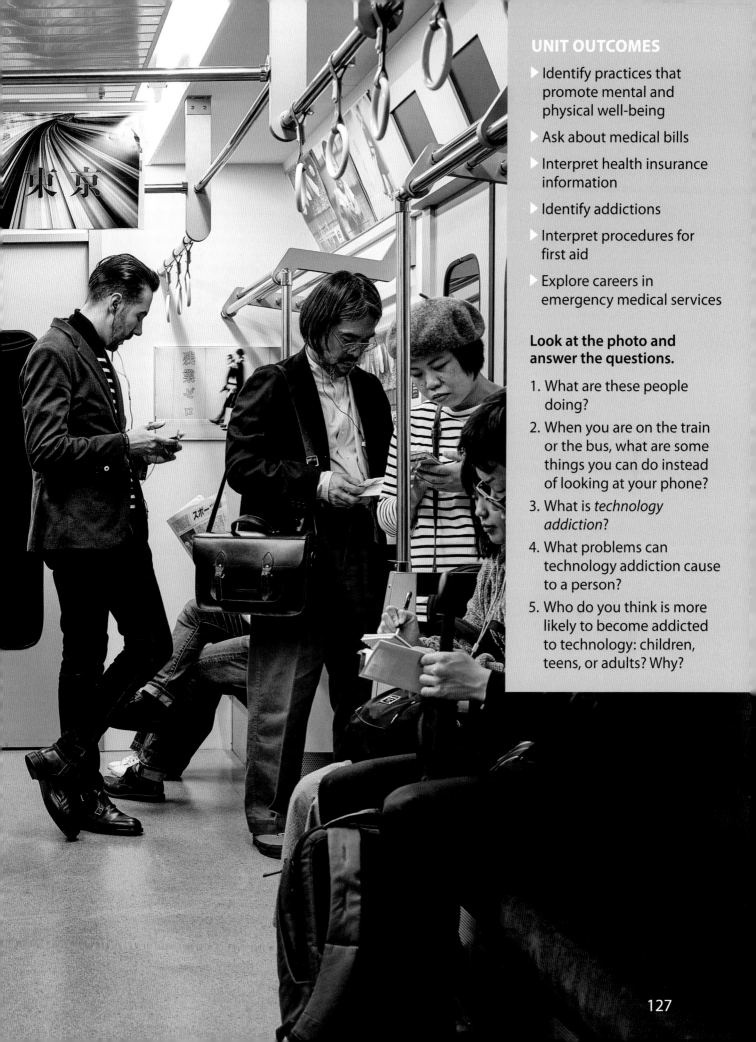

UNIT OUTCOMES

▶ Identify practices that promote mental and physical well-being

▶ Ask about medical bills

▶ Interpret health insurance information

▶ Identify addictions

▶ Interpret procedures for first aid

▶ Explore careers in emergency medical services

Look at the photo and answer the questions.

1. What are these people doing?

2. When you are on the train or the bus, what are some things you can do instead of looking at your phone?

3. What is *technology addiction*?

4. What problems can technology addiction cause to a person?

5. Who do you think is more likely to become addicted to technology: children, teens, or adults? Why?

127

Vocabulary Builder

A A *word family* is a group of words with the same root. The words all have similar meanings but are used as different parts of speech. Look at the example.

Noun(s)	Verb	Adjective
survival, survivor	survive	surviving

- There were no *survivors* of the car accident.
- If cancer is detected early, there is a good chance of *survival*.
- Drugs that dissolve blood clots can help people *survive* heart attacks.
- The *surviving* passengers from the plane crash tried to find help.

B **CLASSIFY** Write the words in the correct columns. Then use a dictionary to find the other forms of each word. Not every word family has every part of speech.

addiction	depressed	insured	poisoning	treat
~~affecting~~	impairment	meditate	tolerance	withdrawal

Noun	Verb	Adjective	Adverb
affect, affection	affect	affecting, affective, affected	affectively

C Choose one of the word families from **B** that has all four parts of speech. Write a sentence using each word form. Use the sentences in **A** as a model.

1. _____

2. _____

3. _____

4. _____

D INFER Each of these expressions is related to health. What do you think each one means? Write your ideas.

1. mental health: _____

2. out of shape: _____

3. self-esteem: _____

4. at risk: _____

E Look at the following questions. Answer the ones you feel comfortable answering.

1. What are the major health care issues facing your community? Which health care issues can be categorized as mental health issues?

_____

_____

2. Do you consider yourself healthy (physically, mentally, spiritually)?

_____

_____

3. Think about people who have high self-esteem. What are their traits? What are the traits of people with low self-esteem?

_____

_____

4. Do you know your family's health history? If so, what health problems have some of your family members faced?

_____

_____

Mind and Body

GOAL ▶ Identify practices that promote mental and physical well-being

A **Discuss the following questions in a small group.**

1. Do you exercise? If so, what type of exercise do you do and how often?

2. Do you eat well? On a scale of one to ten (ten being the healthiest), how healthy are the foods you eat?

3. How could you make your diet healthier?

4. How much water do you drink each day?

5. Do you have a lot of stress in your life? How do you relieve stress?

B **Listen to the following people talk about how they relieve stress. Take notes.** 🎧

Marlie	**Stephanie**	**Fletcher and Katie**
Reason for stress:	Reason for stress:	Reason for stress:
_____	_____	_____
_____	_____	_____
How she relieves stress:	How she relieves stress:	How they relieve stress:
_____	_____	_____
_____	_____	_____

C **Do you identify with any of these people? If yes, in what ways? If not, why not?**

D **Advice is often published online. Read the problems. Do you agree with the advice?**

Ask Ali

1. Dear Ali,
I don't look forward to getting out of bed in the morning. I don't like my job. I don't like to go to school. I don't have any family around, and I have very few friends. I feel like there is no reason to get up in the morning.

-**Unhappy**

Dear Unhappy,

I'm sorry to hear you are feeling that way. Why don't you try doing things that will make you want to get out of bed? Take a nice hot shower, go for a walk, drink some water, eat healthy food. And try to find something that you can look forward to. Every day, add one thing that you enjoy to your day. Maybe learn something new by taking a class. We don't always like what we have to do in life to survive but if you can add at least one or two things to your day that make you happy it will make the rest of your life more enjoyable.

2. Dear Ali,
I'm overweight and out of shape. I can't bear to look at myself in the mirror, and it is really affecting my self-esteem. What can I do?

-**Overweight and Out of Shape**

Dear Overweight and Out of Shape,

I think the best thing you can do for yourself is MOVE. Start by taking a short walk every day and try to increase the time or distance you walk every day. Once you start moving more, you will feel better and it will make you want to eat healthy food. Try to add more vegetables to each meal. These will fill you up and take away the temptation for sugar foods. And drink lots of water. If you get hungry between meals, instead of snacking drink water. Be kind to yourself. This will be a slow and steady process. But if you can keep it up, you will be healthy for the rest of your life.

E **Pretend you are Ali and give advice to the following people.**

1. Dear Ali,
My daughter is a volleyball player and is very lean. She is worried about making it on the team, so she doesn't eat very much. I am worried about her not having enough energy to play, so I've been cooking meals that are high in calories and fat. But she won't eat what I cook. What can I do?—*Mother Without a Clue*

_____

_____

_____

2. Dear Ali,
I have a lot of stress at work. My boss pushes me pretty hard, and I want to do a good job to get ahead, but I never have any time for myself or for my family. The doctor says all the stress is giving me high blood pressure. What should I do?—*Overworked*

_____

_____

_____

F Jada wrote a health-related article for her school paper. Read her article. 🎧

Back on Track

I think I take pretty good care of myself. But it wasn't always that way. I used to work really long hours, eat at fast-food restaurants because they were quick and easy, and I barely ever exercised. But I got a wake-up call from the doctor one day. He said I was obese, at risk for diabetes, and that I might not make it to my fortieth birthday. From that day forward, I began to make changes in my life. I started by going for a walk every day. Now I go to the gym three times a week, walk six miles two days a week, and play volleyball with my family on the weekends. The day the doctor gave me that horrible prognosis, I went straight to the market and filled my cart with healthy food. I now make my lunch every day and cook healthy dinners for my family. My purse and my car are always filled with healthy snacks and water. If I ever get a craving for something really unhealthy, I let myself have one bite of it, and then I stick a piece of gum in my mouth. Although the exercise and eating habits really helped to lower my blood pressure and risk for diabetes, I still have quite a bit of stress in my life. To combat that, I make sure I take at least a half an hour a day for myself. Sometimes I meditate, sometimes I call a good friend, and other times I just sit down and read a book for pleasure.

G Answer the questions.

1. What forced Jada to make changes in her life?

_____

2. What changes did she make?

_____

3. Do you think her article is inspiring? Why?

_____

H CREATE With your classmates, create a health newsletter. Follow the steps.

1. Each student writes a health article that will be inspiring to others who read it.

2. After everyone has finished his or her article, work together to edit the articles.

3. Come up with a title for your newsletter.

4. Put your newsletter together and add artwork and photos.

What's This Charge For?

LESSON 2

GOAL ▸ Ask about medical bills

A Listen to the phone conversation Nadia is having with the receptionist at the doctor's office. Why is Nadia confused about the amount she owes?

DOCTOR
Amy Rosenberg, M.D., Inc.
2880 Chestnut Ave., Ste. 340
Topeka, KS 66675
Office Phone (785) 555-0012

STATEMENT DATE	STATEMENT #	BALANCE DUE
10/06	4689–36	**$20.00**

RESPONSIBLE PARTY
Mrs. Nadia Urich
56 Plains Ave.
Topeka, KS 66675

MAKE CHECK PAYABLE AND REMIT TO
AMY ROSENBERG, M.D., Inc.
2880 Chestnut Ave., Ste. 340
Topeka, KS 66675

PATIENT NAME: Urich, Marina

PROVIDER: Amy Rosenberg, M.D.

DATE	PROCEDURE	DESCRIPTION OF SERVICE	CO-PAY	AMOUNT PAYABLE
8/23	99391	Well-Child Check		$140.00
8/23	90700	DTaP Vaccine		$52.00
8/23	90465	Vaccine Admin		$35.00
8/23	90645	Hib Vaccine		$40.00
8/23	90466	Vaccine Admin		$35.00
8/23		Patient Co-Pay	−$20.00	
9/01		Primary Insurance Payment		−$263.00
9/01		Uncollectible		−$29.00

B Look at the medical bill and answer the questions.

1. Who is expected to pay this bill?

_____

2. Why did the patient go to the doctor?

_____

3. Why is the name of the responsible party different from the patient's name?

_____

4. How much is owed?

_____

5. Does anything on the bill confuse you? Write a question to ask your classmates or teacher.

_____

C Read and listen to this phone conversation. 🎧

Receptionist: Dr. Brook's office.

Patient: Um, yes, this is Maurice Jackson. I came in and saw the doctor a few months ago for the pain I was having in my leg. I just received the bill, and I have a few questions.

Receptionist: Of course, Mr. Jackson. Let me pull up your records. Do you have the date of the statement?

Patient: Yes, it's June 16th.

Receptionist: Ok, I have it here. How can I help you?

Patient: Well, I don't understand what this $264 charge is for.

Receptionist: That is for the X-rays the technician took of your leg.

Patient: OK, but shouldn't my insurance pay for that?

Receptionist: Yes, they might pay some. As you can see on the bill, we have billed your insurance company but are still waiting to hear back from them. Once we do, we'll send you an adjusted bill reflecting how much you owe.

Patient: Oh, so if I don't have to pay this $264, why did you send me a bill?

Receptionist: I know it may seem a bit confusing. Our billing department automatically sends out statements to our current patients every month, whether or not we have heard back from the insurance companies. It usually takes about a month for the bill to reflect what the insurance company has paid, so in general, if you wait two or three months to pay your bill, your statement should show the correct amount due.

Patient: I see. That makes sense. So, I don't need to pay this bill now?

Receptionist: No. Wait until you see an adjusted amount on there and then pay the bill.

Patient: Great! Thanks for your help.

Receptionist: Have a nice day, Mr. Jackson.

D Practice the conversation with a partner. Then switch roles.

E Practice the conversation again. This time use the information in the chart to change the patient's questions. The receptionist will have to be creative to come up with a response.

Name	Reason for Visit	Date of Statement	Question
Jenna Lyn	backache	May 25th	Why isn't the payment I made showing up on the statement?
Javier Bardo	headaches	December 2nd	Do you offer discounted services? I don't have health insurance.
Paula Kofi	skin rash	March 14th	Why do I have to pay more than my co-pay?
Young Lee	ingrown toenail	July 7th	Why didn't my insurance pay for the procedure?

F Look at the bill and write five questions you could ask about it.

STATEMENT		
Skin Care Center 5948 Laredo Street Helena, MT 59626	CLOSING DATE: 7/15 BALANCE DUE: $179.90 ACCOUNT #: 22365-1 AMOUNT ENCLOSED: _____ PATIENT: Katerina Manthos 7653	

Bill to: Katerina Manthos
5948 Laredo Street
Helena, MT 59626

Any change in the above address should be reported to our office.

Skin Care Center
5948 Laredo Street
Helena, MT 59626

DETACH AND RETURN UPPER PORTION WITH YOUR PAYMENT

Keep bottom portion for your records

PATIENT NAME: Katerina Manthos   **PROVIDER:** Elton Frank, M.D.

DATE	CODE	DESCRIPTION	CHARGE	CREDIT
2/05	99204	Office Visit New Patient	**$240.00**	
		Paid By Health Care PPO		$240.00
6/15	11301	Shave Skin Lesion 0.6-1.0cm	**$474.00**	
		Paid By Health Care PPO		$320.00
6/15	88305	Tissue Exam by Pathologist	**$565.00**	
		Paid By Health Care PPO		$420.00
6/15	A4550	Surgical Tray	**$75.00**	
		Paid By Health Care PPO		$75.00
		DUE FROM PATIENT	**$299.00**	

1. _____

2. _____

3. _____

4. _____

5. _____

G Go over the bill with your teacher to make sure you understand everything on it.

H Find a partner (receptionist) and have a conversation, asking him or her the questions you wrote in **F.** Then switch roles.

Health Insurance

GOAL ▶ Interpret health insurance information

A How much do you know about health insurance? In a small group, try to answer the following questions. If you need help, talk to other groups.

1. Is it mandatory in your state to have health insurance?

2. What happens if you see a doctor or go to a hospital without health insurance?

3. What is the difference between an HMO and a PPO?

B Look at the graph about insured and uninsured people and answer the questions.

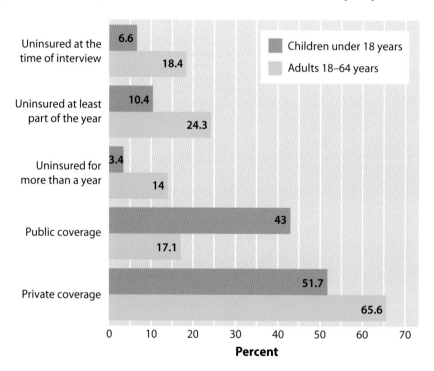

1. What is the percentage of insured adults? _____

2. What is the percentage of children who were uninsured for more than a year? _____

3. What is the percentage of adults who have private insurance? _____

4. What is the percentage of children who have public coverage? _____

C Ask your partner questions about the information in the graph in **B**. Use the questions from **B** as examples.

D Look at the graph about uninsured people and complete the sentences.

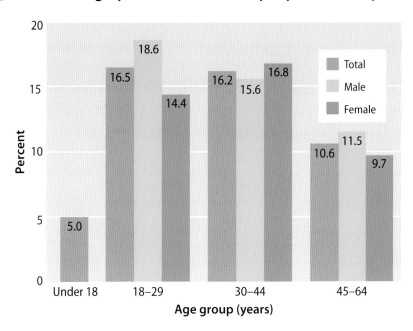

1. Of both sexes, the _____ are the less insured.

2. Out of all the age groups, the _____ -year-olds are the less insured.

3. _____ of children are uninsured.

4. _____ of children are insured.

5. _____ of women aged 30–44 are uninsured.

6. _____ of people in my age group are uninsured.

E ANALYZE Write five more sentences about the statistics in the chart in D.

1. _____

2. _____

3. _____

4. _____

5. _____

F Read the chart about insurance coverage and demographics. Then write six questions based on the data.

	Uninsured at the Time of Interview	Public Health Plan Coverage	Private Health Insurance Coverage
Race / Ethnicity			
Hispanic	29.7%	22.7%	48.7%
White only	9.1%	17.3%	76.3%
Black only	14.5%	33.8%	55.2%
Asian only	8.8%	16.1%	76.2%
Other and multiple races	19.1%	32.2%	52.3%
Education			
Less than high school	31.6%	38.5%	32.4%
High school diploma or GED	18.2%	25.8%	58.6%
Some College	12.5%	22.4%	68.6%
Bachelor's Degree or More	5.3%	8.9%	87.6%

1. _____

2. _____

3. _____

4. _____

5. _____

6. _____

G Ask three classmates the questions you wrote in **F.**

H GRAPH In a small group, choose one of the two graphs or the chart presented in this lesson. Recreate the data using information from the students in your class.

Addictions

GOAL ▶ Identify addictions

A **Look up the word *addiction* in a dictionary. Write the definition and an example sentence that uses the word.**

addiction *n.* _____

_____

_____

B **Work with a partner and brainstorm a list of addictions.**

C **Match the words to their correct definitions and write the complete sentences on a separate piece of paper. Use a dictionary if you need to.**

_____ 1. Tolerance is . . .

_____ 2. Impairment is . . .

_____ 3. Substance addiction is . . .

_____ 4. Physiological dependence is . . .

_____ 5. A twelve-step program is . . .

_____ 6. Psychological dependence is . . .

_____ 7. Process addiction is . . .

_____ 8. Detoxification is . . .

_____ 9. Withdrawal is . . .

_____ 10. An addict is . . .

a. the process of giving up a substance or activity to which a person has become addicted.

b. a condition in which a person is dependent on some chemical substance.

c. a plan for overcoming an addiction by going through twelve stages of personal development.

d. a condition in which a person requires certain activities or the intake of some substance in order to maintain mental stability.

e. a condition in which a person is dependent on some type of behavior.

f. an inability to carry on normal, everyday functions because of an addiction.

g. the ability of the body to endure a certain amount of a substance.

h. the process of adjusting to the absence of some substance or activity that a person has become addicted to.

i. a person physically or emotionally dependent on a substance or an activity.

j. a condition in which a person's body requires certain behaviors or the intake of some substance, without which it will become physically ill.

D Look at the list of addictions. Choose which ones are substance (*S*) addictions and which ones are process (*P*) addictions.

1. alcohol   S   P
2. caffeine   S   P
3. food   S   P
4. gambling   S   P

5. illegal drugs   S   P
6. prescription medicine   S   P
7. shopping   S   P
8. smoking (nicotine)   S   P

9. technology   S   P
10. video games   S   P
11. work   S   P

E In a small group, discuss the following questions.

1. Why do people become addicts?

2. What can you do if you are addicted to something?

3. What can you do to help a friend or family member who is addicted to something?

F **ANALYZE** Read the statements. Do you think each person has an addiction? Choose *yes* or *no* and give a reason for each answer.

1. Although my uncle Gerry sold his car to spend more time at casinos in Las Vegas, he says he doesn't have a gambling problem.
   Addiction: yes no **Reason:** _____

2. Even though her sister spends thousands of dollars a month on her credit cards, she doesn't think she is a shopaholic.
   Addiction: yes no **Reason:** _____

3. In spite of the fact that Fletcher plays video games for three hours a night instead of doing his homework, he denies he has a problem.
   Addiction: yes no **Reason:** _____

4. Danielle is convinced she isn't addicted to caffeine although she has to drink two cups of coffee before she can get out of bed in the morning.
   Addiction: yes no **Reason:** _____

Technology addiction can be dangerous and affect your performance at work or school.

G Study the chart.

Adverb Clauses of Concession	
Dependent clause	**Independent clause**
Although he spends a lot of time in Las Vegas,	he says he doesn't have a gambling problem.
Even though her sister spends thousands of dollars a month,	she doesn't think she is a shopaholic.
Though she has to drink two cups of coffee before she can get out of bed in the morning,	she is convinced she isn't addicted to caffeine.
In spite of the fact that he plays video games for three hours a night,	he denies he has a problem.
Explanation: Adverb clauses of concession show a contrast in ideas. The main or independent clauses show the unexpected outcome. The unexpected outcome in the third example is that it is surprising that she thinks she isn't addicted to caffeine. **Note:** The clauses can be reversed and have the same meaning. Do not use a comma if the independent clause comes first in the sentence. **Example:** *She doesn't think she is a shopaholic even though she spends thousands of dollars a month.*	

H Write sentences with dependent and independent clauses. Use these ideas and the sentences in the chart in **G** as examples.

technology addiction / spends five hours a day online
shopping addiction / goes to the mall at least once a day
food addiction / weighs over 300 pounds
drug addiction / sold all his devices to buy more drugs

1. _____

_____

2. _____

_____

3. _____

_____

4. _____

_____

I VISUALIZE Imagine a good friend has an addiction to something. In your notebook, write about his or her addiction. How is it affecting your friend's life? How is it affecting your life? How is your friendship different because of it?

First Aid

GOAL ▶ Interpret procedures for first aid

A **LABEL VISUALS** What does a first-aid kit have in it? Use the words in the box to label each item. Write the number in the picture.

1. adhesive bandages	6. cold compress / ice pack	11. scissors
2. adhesive cloth tape	7. compress dressing	12. sterile gauze pads
3. antibiotic ointment	8. first-aid manual	13. sterile gloves
4. antiseptic wipes	9. hydrocortisone ointment	14. thermometer
5. aspirin	10. roller bandage	15. tweezers

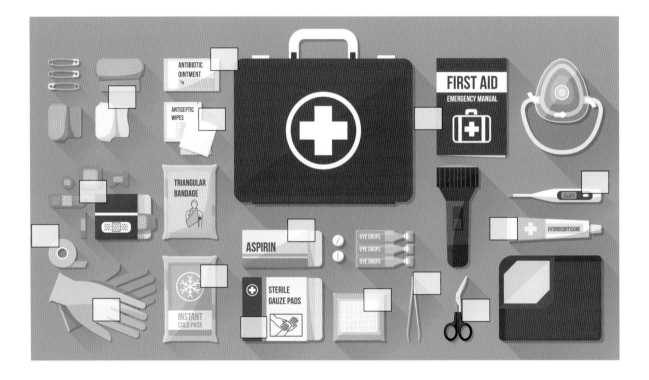

B Do you have a first-aid kit? Why is each item important? Discuss your ideas with your classmates.

C Define the following injuries.

1. burn: _____

2. choking: _____

3. poisoning: _____

4. open wound: _____

5. head injury: _____

6. shock: _____

D Look at the list of first-aid procedures. Write the injury from **C** that corresponds to each item.

1. Call 911.

   choking, poisoning, head injury, shock _____

2. Call Poison Control.

   _____

3. Control external bleeding.

   _____

4. Cover with a light gauze dressing.

   _____

5. Have the person lie down.

   _____

6. Help maintain body temperature.

   _____

7. Perform the Heimlich maneuver.

   _____

8. Stop the bleeding with a piece of sterile gauze.

   _____

9. Strike the victim's back between the shoulder blades five times.

   _____

10. Treat wounds.

   _____

E Read the information. Compare it with your answers in **D**. Were you right? Make a note of any difficult vocabulary and discuss as a class.

First-Aid Procedures*		
Injury	**Do**	**Don't**
burn	Run cold water over burn area for 15 minutes. Cover the burn with a light gauze dressing. If blisters pop, apply a light antibiotic ointment and cover with light gauze dressing.	**Don't** put any creams or greases on the burned area. **Don't** pop any blisters. **Don't** use an ice pack.
choking	Call 911. Strike the victim's back between the shoulder blades five times. Perform Heimlich maneuver.	**Don't** give water to the person.
poisoning	Call 911 if the person is unconscious or having trouble breathing. Call Poison Control (800-222-1222).	**Don't** induce vomiting. **Don't** give the person anything to eat or drink.
open wound	Stop the bleeding with a piece of sterile gauze. Wash with soap and water (if minor), apply a thin layer of antibiotic ointment, and cover with a bandage.	**Don't** remove any object protruding from injury. **Don't** wash or apply ointment to a large, deep wound.
head injury	Call 911 if the person is unconscious or drowsy. Treat wounds. Ice a small bump.	**Don't** leave the person alone, especially when sleeping. Instead, wake up every two to three hours and have the person answer simple questions.
shock	Call 911. Have the person lie down. Control external bleeding. Help maintain body temperature.	**Don't** raise the person's head. **Don't** give the person food or drink.

* Not all first-aid procedures for each injury are listed.

F APPLY Divide the class into "victims" and "good citizens." All victims should write an injury from **D** on a piece of paper and show it to a good citizen. Good citizens should offer advice.

EXAMPLE:

Victim: (shows Good Citizen card that reads *Choking*)

Good Citizen: I'm going to call 911. Then I'm going to strike your back five times between your shoulder blades. If that doesn't work, I'm going to perform the Heimlich maneuver. I will not give you water.

LESSON
6

Explore the Workforce

GOAL ▶ Explore careers in emergency medical services

A When you or someone you know is experiencing a medical emergency, who do you call? Who will administer emergency care?

B The basic differences between an EMT and a paramedic are the level of education, hours of training, and the types of procedures they are allowed to perform. Read the table.

Emergency Medical Technician (EMT)	Paramedic
• provide basic medical care to patients in the field, including stopping external bleeding, applying neck braces, and administering CPR • have CPR certification • complete a 1–2 year EMT program to learn how to assess, care for, and transport patients • complete 120 to 150 hours of training • pass the National Registry of Emergency Medical Technicians (NREMT) exam	• provide advanced medical care in the field, such as administering medication, inserting IVs, and resuscitating patients • have CPR certification • complete a 1–2 year EMT program to learn how to assess, care for, and transport patients • obtain a 2-year Associate degree to learn more advanced procedures • complete 1,200 to 1,800 hours of training • pass the National Registry of Emergency Medical Technicians (NREMT) exam • pass the National Registry Paramedic Cognitive exam

C Write *EMT*, *paramedic* or *both* on the line that follows each statement.

1. must pass the NREMT exam to become certified _____

2. completes 1,200-1,800 hours of training _____

3. must get CPR certified _____

4. completes 120 to 150 hours of training _____

5. provides advanced medical care to patients in the field _____

6. provides basic medical care to patients in the field _____

7. must pass the National Registry Paramedic Cognitive exam _____

8. can insert an IV _____

9. completes a 1–2 year EMT program _____

10. has an Associate degree _____

D Write one sentence that explains the differences between an EMT and a paramedic.

_____

_____

E Based on the information presented in the table in **B**, who do you think makes more money, an EMT or a paramedic? Why?

_____

_____

F **ANALYZE** Look at the bar graph and discuss the questions.

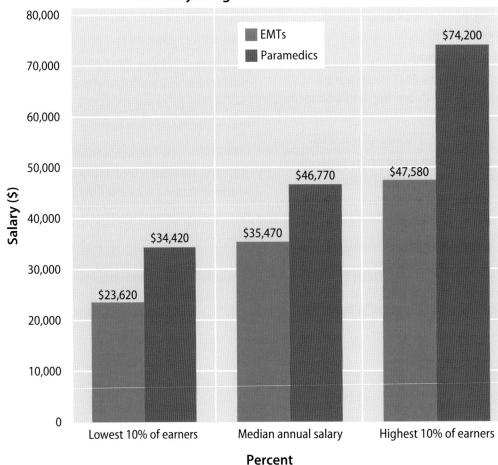

Salary Ranges for EMTs and Paramedics

1. Overall, who makes more money: EMTs or paramedics? Why do you think this is so?

2. What factors do you think contribute to the difference in salary range? Brainstorm with a partner.

G One of the factors that contributes to a difference in salary range is geographical location. Read the statements and fill in the state names.

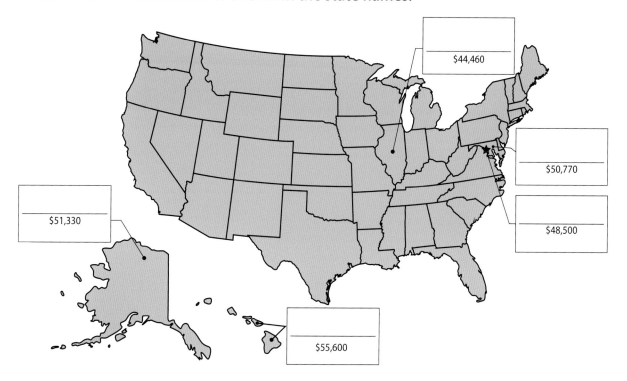

$44,460

$50,770

$51,330

$48,500

$55,600

1. Hawaii has the highest paid EMTs.

2. EMTs in the District of Columbia make more than those in Illinois.

3. EMTs in Maryland make more than those in the District of Columbia.

4. The median salary for EMTs in Illinois is $44,460.

5. Alaska has the second highest-paid EMTs.

H What do you think it's like to be an EMT? Listen to Felix Hernandez, an EMT and instructor, talk about his experiences in this podcast.

I On a separate piece of paper, write down some ideas that you heard.

1. How many hours does an EMT work?

2. Do you ever get bored?

3. What are the most common types of calls an EMT gets?

4. What is the best part of being an EMT?

5. What is the worst thing about being an EMT?

J With a partner, role-play the interview you heard using the questions and your notes from above.

Review

A **Write one healthy solution for each problem.**

1. Problem: I eat fast food three times a week because I have no time to cook.

   Solution: _____

2. Problem: I have high blood pressure, and I am at risk for diabetes.

   Solution: _____

3. Problem: I am really stressed at work.

   Solution: _____

4. Problem: My children are overweight.

   Solution: _____

B **Read the bill and write four questions you would ask about it.**

	PATIENT NAME: Claudio Tovar		PROVIDER NAME: Lalita Kanne, M.D.		
DATE	**PROCEDURE**	**DESCRIPTION OF SERVICE**	**CO-PAY**	**AMOUNT PAYABLE**	
8/23	99391	Well-Child Check		$150.00	
8/23	90700	DTaP Vaccine		$52.00	
8/23	90465	Vaccine Admin		$38.00	
8/23	90645	Hib Vaccine		$55.00	
8/23	90466	Vaccine Admin		$38.00	
8/23		Patient Co-Pay	−$25.00		
9/17		Primary Insurance Payment		−$250.00	
9/17		Uncollectible		−$58.00	
			AMOUNT DUE: $0.00		

1. _____

2. _____

3. _____

4. _____

Learner Log	I can identify practices that promote mental and physical well-being. ☐ Yes ☐ No ☐ Maybe	I can ask about medical bills. ☐ Yes ☐ No ☐ Maybe

148   UNIT 5

C Work with a partner and have a conversation between a patient and a person at the doctor's office with the questions you wrote. Then switch roles.

D Read the bar graph about health insurance coverage and answer the questions.

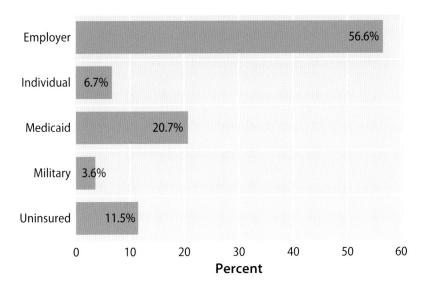

1. What is the percentage of adults who are uninsured? _____

2. What is the percentage of adults who are insured by their employers? _____

3. What is the percentage of adults who are on Medicaid? _____

4. What is the percentage of adults who have insurance coverage? _____

E On a separate piece of paper, write sentences combining these ideas.

EXAMPLE: nicotine addiction / smokes two packs of cigarettes a day

Even though he smokes two packs of cigarettes a day, he doesn't think he is addicted to nicotine.

1. exercise addiction / works out 3 times a day

2. sleeping addiction / sleeps 11 hours a night

3. food addiction / eats all day long

4. coffee addiction / drinks 4 cups a day

F Write down six injuries you learned about in this unit. In a group, discuss the first-aid procedures for each one.

_____   _____   _____

_____   _____   _____

Learner Log	I can interpret health insurance information.	I can identify addictions.	I can interpret procedures for first aid.
	Yes No Maybe	Yes No Maybe	Yes No Maybe

Vocabulary Review

A **Choose the correct word for each sentence.**

1. _____ helps me relax when I've had a long day at work.

   a. Detoxification   b. Meditation   c. Tolerance   d. Depression

2. They think she has a sleeping pill _____.

   a. process   b. insurance   c. depression   d. addiction

3. If you are with someone who is in _____, you should call 911.

   a. shock   b. out of shape   c. meditation   d. treatment

4. How would you _____ someone who has a head injury?

   a. affect   b. treat   c. impair   d. insure

5. Jared's body has built up a _____ to alcohol since he has been drinking for so long.

   a. tolerance   b. substance   c. detoxification   d. withdrawal

B **Give two examples of each of these items.**

1. Substance addictions: _____ _____

2. Process addictions: _____ _____

3. First-aid kit items: _____ _____

4. Items on a medical bill: _____ _____

C **Write sentences using each of these terms.**

1. uninsured: _____

2. at risk: _____

3. self-esteem: _____

4. responsible party: _____

5. survive: _____

Health Presentation
SOFT SKILL ▶ Presentation Skills

Presentation Topics

- Healthy Practices
- Medical Bills
- Health Insurance
- Addictions
- First Aid

1. Form a team of four or five students. Decide which topic your team will work on. (Each team should choose a different topic.)

2. Choose positions for each member of your team.

Position	Job Description	Student Name
Student 1: Project Leader	Check that everyone speaks English. Check that everyone participates.	
Student 2: Secretary	Take notes on your team's ideas.	
Student 3: Coordinator	Divide presentation into parts. Assign each team member one part of presentation.	
Student 4: Director	Organize presentation so that individual parts create a unified whole.	
Student 5: Member	Do assigned part of presentation. Supportively critique other members' work as they rehearse their parts of presentation.	

3. Gather information for your presentation from this unit and other sources.

4. Decide how to present your material creatively.

5. Create any materials needed for your presentation.

6. Practice your presentation.

7. Give your presentation to the class.

PRESENTATION SKILLS:
Make it interesting

Make your presentation more interesting by presenting your information in a unique way. Have each person do something different with the information. Some ideas: take a class poll, do a role play, play music, teach a chant, call on the audience to answer questions, etc.

Reading Challenge

A Plants are a very important part of Grace Gobbo's work. In a group, discuss the different uses of plants.

B Natural remedies are non-manufactured medicines that can cure illnesses. Make a list of natural remedies that you know of.

Remedy	Illness it cures

C Read about Grace Gobbo, ethnobotanist.

D SUMMARIZE Complete each sentence with what you learned from the reading.

1. The people of Tanzania don't use imported pharmaceuticals because _____.

   _____

2. Grace wanted to learn more about traditional healing, so she _____.

   _____

3. The secrets of traditional healers are dying with them because _____.

   _____

4. Medical plants in Tanzania are disappearing because _____.

   _____

5. Grace believes that people will make better choices if they _____.

   _____

Grace Gobbo

Disappearing Knowledge

For many people in Tanzania, imported pharmaceuticals are too expensive. For centuries, this east African country has had traditional healers who use locally grown medicinal plants to help treat sick people, so the high price of imported drugs wasn't a problem. Unfortunately, this indigenous medical knowledge is disappearing and so are the plants. Grace Gobbo is an
5 ethnobotanist who hopes to change that.

Initially, Grace didn't believe in traditional healing because her father was a medical doctor. But once she began studying botany, she learned about plants that had successfully treated coughs and stopped bacterial infections. Wanting to know more, Grace started interviewing traditional healers, who had endless accounts of plants being used to treat skin and chest
10 infections, diabetes, stomach ulcers, heart disease, and even mental illness. "Before now, these facts existed only as an oral tradition," she explains. "Nothing was written down. The knowledge is literally dying out with the elders since today's young generation considers natural remedies old-fashioned." Grace hopes that, by creating a record of these natural remedies, she can educate other young people about the possibility of using these plants to cure ailments.

15 In addition to the traditional healers' knowledge dying out, medicinal plants are disappearing due to farming, mining, and other development. Plant products are used for fuel by most of the people in Tanzania, and agriculture is a major part of their economy. But Grace still believes people will ultimately do what is right. "I believe in people. I think if they learn and understand the value of the environment, they will make better choices. If they knew the plants
20 they cut down could help their children recover from illness, they might reconsider. Loggers might give healers a chance to collect tree bark at the same time wood is harvested. We're working hard to bring information about sustainable agriculture and forest management to the public and show them how to apply it."

6 Retail

UNIT OUTCOMES

▶ Do product research

▶ Purchase goods and services by phone and online

▶ Interpret product guarantees and warranties

▶ Return a product

▶ Sell a product

▶ Explore the role of a customer service representative

Look at the photo and answer the questions.

1. This is a display at a home electronics and appliances trade fair in Berlin, Germany. What products do you see in the photo?

2. What other types of products do you expect to see at a fair like this one?

3. What do you think the people in the photo are doing at this fair?

Vocabulary Builder

A Using the terms in the box, discuss the picture with a partner. Look up any terms you do not know in a dictionary.

EXAMPLE: The woman is asking the salesperson about the product warranty.

convince	guarantee	policy	refund	review
exchange	make	quality	research	transaction
free of charge	model	receipt	return	warranty

B With your partner, write a story on a separate piece of paper about one of the customers in the picture. Use as many of the words from the box in **A** as possible. Be prepared to share your story with the class. Make sure to answer these questions in your story: What is the customer looking for? Why did the customer(s) come to this store? What is the outcome of their shopping experience?

C CLASSIFY Look at the unit outcomes. Then look back at the terms in **A**. Decide which terms go with each outcome. (Some words and phrases can be used with more than one outcome.)

1. Do product research: _____

2. Purchase goods and services: _____

3. Interpret product guarantees and warranties: _____

4. Return a product: _____

5. Sell a product: _____

6. Explore the role of a customer service representative: _____

D Knowing a synonym for an unfamiliar word will often help you better understand its meaning. Find synonyms for these words in a dictionary or thesaurus.

Word	Synonym
allege	
conform	
convince	
exchange	
fault	
guarantee	
malfunction	
model	
quality	
refund	
research	
return	
review	

How Much Is It?

GOAL ▶ Do product research

A Imagine that you are going to buy these products. In a group, discuss what information you need to research before you make your purchases. Write your ideas next to each item.

1. bed: _____

2. refrigerator: _____

3. television: _____

4. cell phone / smartphone: _____

5. air conditioner: _____

6. car: _____

B Listen to the conversation Maya is having with the salesperson. What does she want to know about the patio set? Write her questions. 🎧

1. _____

2. _____

3. _____

4. _____

5. _____

6. _____

7. _____

8. _____

C How did the salesperson answer the questions in B? Discuss the answers with your classmates.

D Look at the list of ways to research a product. Which methods have you used before?

- Ask friends and family
- Ask a salesperson
- Go online and read product reviews
- Read a consumer magazine

E Maya went online to research the patio furniture she saw in the store. Read the product reviews she found. 🎧

Acme Furniture Patio Set $1,450

Customer Reviews

***** **Good-looking, but poor quality**
The cushions are almost flat after a few sittings. The fabric started pilling, and I thought we could remove the fabric to wash it, but that's not the case. It stains easily. Not for outdoors or indoors. Not worth spending your money on.

***** **Not for outdoors**
This set is NOT for outdoor use. We bought this set in June, and by the end of the summer it looked TERRIBLE. Our patio gets late afternoon sun, and after a month the wood stain started to fade. We are going to stain it with deck stain to try to make it last another year. For the amount we paid, we are very disappointed in the quality.

***** **Love it!**
I bought this set in May and absolutely LOVE it! It is under a gazebo and gets wet from the rain, but I haven't had the splitting or mold that the other people are talking about. If it rains, you just have to put the seat cushions up so they can dry … simple. It's comfortable, and I would buy it again! Maybe some other people got a "bad batch" or something. Love it!

***** **You get what you pay for**
I got this beautiful set for our open-air, roofless patio about three weeks ago. So far, it has endured the weather, but the wood is too thin to endure year-round exposure. Even the owner's manual suggests covering it when not in use. Our plan is to enjoy it now and stash it away in the garage after the summer. This set was on sale at the time we made the purchase, and I'm glad I didn't pay full price. If you want to worry less about your wood furniture, spend a little more for heavier woods. I would give five stars for the "look" and two stars for "quality." If we had paid full price for this set, it would have made its way back to the store.

F Based on the reviews in **E**, would you buy the patio furniture if it were on sale? Why?

_____

_____

G Which review made the biggest impression on you? Why?

_____

_____

H Think of something you have bought recently. Write a review for it on a separate piece of paper.

I Imagine that you are buying a new cell phone. What questions would you ask before you made your decision to purchase a particular model?

1. _____

2. _____

3. _____

J Think about your current cell phone. Answer the questions.

1. What is the make and model? _____

2. How much did it cost? _____

3. Where did you buy it? _____

4. How is the quality? _____

5. Have you ever had any problems with it? _____

6. Did it come with a warranty? _____

7. What do you like about it? _____

8. What do you not like about it? _____

K **RESEARCH** Talk to your classmates to learn about different cell phones. Ask them the questions in I and J.

L Based on your product research, what kind of cell phone would you buy?

_____

M **RESEARCH** Choose one of the items in **A** to purchase. Do product research by reading reviews online or talking to your classmates. What did you find out about this product? Write some of the things you learned.

_____

_____

_____

_____

_____

Shopping Online

GOAL ▶ Purchase goods and services by phone and online

A Take a class poll. How many of your classmates shop online? How many of your classmates prefer to shop in person?

B Look at the page from a housewares catalog. Underline these pieces of information for each product: item name, item description, item price, and item number.

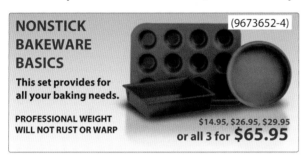

NONSTICK BAKEWARE BASICS
(9673652-4)

This set provides for all your baking needs.

PROFESSIONAL WEIGHT
WILL NOT RUST OR WARP

$14.95, $26.95, $29.95
or all 3 for **$65.95**

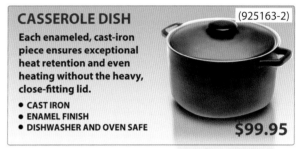

CASSEROLE DISH
(925163-2)

Each enameled, cast-iron piece ensures exceptional heat retention and even heating without the heavy, close-fitting lid.

● CAST IRON
● ENAMEL FINISH
● DISHWASHER AND OVEN SAFE

$99.95

SILVER- DOLLAR PANCAKE PAN
(986534-9)

Cook up perfect little silver-dollar pancakes in this heavy-gauge aluminum pan with a nonstick interior.

● EASY CLEAN
● RECIPE INCLUDED
● DISHWASHER SAFE

$39.95

WOK SET
(9693312-4)

Stay-cool bamboo handles and knobs add natural accents. Universal usage includes stir-frying sautéing, deep-frying, steaming, and parboiling.

● COLD-ROLLED CARBON STEEL
● HAND WASH

$74.95

EVERLAST STAINLESS SAUTÉ PAN
(9132456-5)

This stainless cookware is perfect for everyday use with traditional electric or gas ranges. The pure aluminum core covers the bottom of the pan and also extends up the sides. This provides superior heat conductivity as well as even heat distribution.

● BEAUTIFULLY POLISHED, MAGNETIC STAINLESS STEEL EXTERIOR LAYER
● STAY-COOL, CAST STAINLESS STEEL HANDLES
● TIGHT-FITTING STAINLESS STEEL LID LOCKS IN FLAVOR AND HEAT
● OVEN SAFE TO 500 DEGREES
● DISHWASHER SAFE

$149.95

C Listen to four conversations between salespeople and customers who are buying items they saw online. Complete the table based on what you hear. 🎧

	Item	Total Cost	Method of Payment
1.			
2.			
3.			
4.			

D With your teacher, review the process of making a purchase online. Look for each step in the screen shots.

1. Find the website you want to buy something from.

2. Perform a search.

3. Look at the results of your search.

4. Narrow down the results to one item.

5. Make your purchase.

E In a group, discuss the pros and cons of buying something online. Make two lists on a separate piece of paper.

F What goods or services do you like to buy online? _____

_____

G With a partner, create a list of specific items to sell in a catalog or online.

1. Decide what types of items you could sell.

2. On a separate piece of paper, create art, descriptions, and prices for at least five items.

H Exchange papers with another pair of students. Have a conversation about purchasing the new items with your partner. One of you should be a sales representative explaining your products. Sit back-to-back to simulate selling and purchasing on the phone.

I Search online for items similar to the ones on the catalog page in **B**. Follow the steps in **D** to find the items you want. If you don't have computer access, answer the questions.

1. What would you like to buy online? _____

2. What words will you type in to search for the item? _____

3. Do you know of an online store that sells the item? _____

4. Once you click on the store that sells your item, what information will you look for?

_____

5. How will you decide if you are going to purchase the item? What information will you consider?

_____

Life
ONLINE

Be careful when purchasing online with a credit card.
1. Make sure you always see a lock 🔒 in the browser bar to make sure that your information will be protected.
2. Another way to purchase safely online is to store your credit card information with a third-party website, and click on that site to make the purchase.
3. If you do use a credit card, always use the same card for online purchases. That way if you do have a problem or someone gets your information, you only have one credit card company to deal with.

Is This Under Warranty?

GOAL ▶ Interpret product guarantees and warranties

A **Discuss these situations with a partner and make decisions.**

What would you do if . . .

1. you wanted to start up your new laptop and it didn't work?

2. your phone stopped working one week after you bought it?

3. your new bluetooth speaker didn't work?

4. you washed a new shirt according to the care instructions on the tag and it shrank?

B **A *warranty* or *guarantee* is a written promise by a company to replace or repair a product free of charge within a certain time period after purchase if it has any defects. Read this warranty for a bluetooth speaker.** 🎧

The warranty on the electronic components in this bluetooth speaker remains in effect for one year from the date of purchase. This warranty protects the original owner and all subsequent owners, provided that the product was purchased from an authorized dealer. A copy of the original dated bill of sale must be presented whenever warranty service is required.

This warranty covers all defects in material and workmanship. The following are not covered: damage caused by accident, misuse, abuse, product modification, or neglect; damage from failure to follow instructions contained in the instruction manual. We reserve the right to replace a discontinued model with a comparable model. If you require warranty service, please visit our website and fill out a warranty request.

C **Answer these questions about the warranty in B.**

1. How do you get your speaker repaired or replaced?

_____

2. How long is the speaker guaranteed for?

_____

3. Who does the warranty protect?

_____

4. Does the warranty cover you if you drop and break the speaker?

_____

D Warranties are often difficult to understand because they are worded in legal language.

> Seller warrants to the original customers purchasing products from Seller that all such products, under normal use and operation, will be free from defects in materials and workmanship affecting form, fit, and function.

In other words . . .

The seller says that if I use this product under normal conditions, as it was meant to be used, there won't be any problems with it.

E **RESTATE** With a partner, restate each sentence in your own words.

1. Any claims alleging failure of products to conform to the foregoing warranty may be made only by the customer who purchased the product.

   _____

   _____

2. The foregoing warranty only applies while the product is being used in the original machine with the original hardware and software configuration.

   _____

   _____

3. Seller, at its option, will repair, replace, or provide a credit or refund of either the original purchase price less a restock fee or current fair market value, whichever is less, for any product Seller deems to be defective.

   _____

   _____

4. The above warranties cover only defects arising under normal use and do not include malfunctions or failures from misuse, neglect, alteration, abuse, improper installation, or acts of nature.

   _____

   _____

5. Removal of the labeling on products will void all warranties.

   _____

   _____

F Read the guarantee from a printer company.

OUR NO-HASSLE GUARANTEE

Our products are backed the way they are built—the best in the industry. Our no-hassle printer guarantee gives you excellent product support with no worries. Now you can enjoy the benefit of a substitute printer if your printer fails during the first year of use.

We will send a replacement printer to you within 48 hours of your request for any printer that fails to meet the factory specifications or fails to power up within one year of your invoice date. Upon receipt of your no-hassle replacement printer, you must return your defective printer to us. Your defective printer will be exchanged for the same make and model, or for a printer of equal value. In addition, if your printer has three separate quality issues which are documented with our technical support team within one year from the date of your invoice, we will permanently replace your defective printer with a new printer of equal or greater value.

G Choose the best answer.

1. You can receive a replacement printer if your printer doesn't work during the first . . .

   a. 48 hours.　　　　　b. year.　　　　　c. week.

2. How soon will a replacement printer be sent?

   a. within 48 hours　　b. within one year　　c. within one week

3. When you receive your replacement printer, you must . . .

   a. return the defective printer.　　b. do nothing.　　c. call the company.

4. If you have three problems with your printer during the first year, the company will . . .

   a. fix your printer for free.　　b. refund your money.　　c. permanently replace the printer.

H With a partner, choose a product from the list and write your own warranty or guarantee. Use the ideas from the warranties and guarantees you have read in this lesson, but use your own words.

bicycle　　　　cell phone / smartphone　　　　digital camera　　　　washing machine

Returns and Exchanges

LESSON 4

GOAL ▶ Return a product

A Think of a product you have returned to the store where you bought it. What did you return and why? Discuss your experience with your classmates.

B Read and listen to the conversation. 🎧

Sales Associate: Can I help you with something?

Customer: Yes, I'd like to return these shoes. I wore them around my house on the carpet for a few days and they are still uncomfortable. The salesman who sold them to me insisted they would stretch out and soften up, but they haven't. I'd like to get my money back.

Sales Associate: I'm afraid I can't give you your money back. These were on sale and we don't offer refunds for sale items.

Customer: Can I exchange them?

Sales Associate: Yes, you can exchange them for something of equal value.

Customer: OK, I'll do that. Let me look around for a bit.

Sales Associate: Take your time.

C Listen to each question and write the answer. 🎧

1. _____

2. _____

3. _____

4. _____

5. _____

6. _____

Life ONLINE   If you want to return something you bought online, you can call the company or go through their website. Most of the time, there is a return link that you can click on to start the process. You will need your email address and order number. At the end of the process, they will either give you a mailing label to print out and affix to the box or they will email you a QR code for the shipping company to scan.

D **Read the return and price policies and the statements. Choose *T* (true) or *F* (false).**

Thank you for shopping at Nico's. Return or exchange for merchandise within two weeks with tags attached and / or in original packaging. Original sales receipt is required for full refund. Final sale on all sale items.

1. You can exchange sale items.	T	F
2. You need an original sales receipt for a refund.	T	F

Valid photo ID required for all returns (except for credit card purchases), exchanges, and to receive and redeem store credit. With a receipt, a full refund in the original form of payment will be issued for new and unread books and unopened music within four days. For merchandise purchased with a gift card, a store credit will be issued. Without an original receipt, a store credit issued by mail will be offered at the current price. With a receipt, returns of new and unread books and unopened music from our website can be made for store credit. Textbooks after 14 days or without a receipt are not returnable. Used books are not returnable.

3. If you pay with a gift card you can get cash back.	T	F
4. You cannot return used books.	T	F
5. If you have a receipt, you can get a refund on unopened music within four days.	T	F
6. If you don't have a receipt, you can exchange an item.	T	F

All returns and exchanges must be new, unused, and have original packaging and accessories. Some items cannot be returned if opened. For our full return and exchange policy, visit the store or log onto our website. For a gift receipt, bring this receipt back to any store within 90 days. Ask about receipt look-up.

7. All opened items can be exchanged.	T	F

We will not be undersold. Guaranteed! If you find a lower price at any of our competitors, we will meet that price.

8. This store will offer you a lower price than its competitors.	T	F

E **Look back at all the false statements in D. On a separate piece of paper, rewrite each statement correctly.**

F Listen to six conversations and write the corresponding conversation number. Then write *returned* or *exchanged*. 🎧

Conversation #	Reason for returning or exchanging item	Was item returned or exchanged?
	bought the wrong package	
	already have them	
	bad reception	
	don't fit right	
	broken	
	doesn't work with computer	

G Write two reasons you might return each of the items.

1. digital video camera

    a. _____   b. _____

2. gallon of milk

    a. _____   b. _____

3. pair of pants

    a. _____   b. _____

4. laptop computer

    a. _____   b. _____

5. sunglasses

    a. _____   b. _____

6. textbook

    a. _____   b. _____

H ROLE-PLAY In pairs, pretend you are in a store. One student is the clerk and the other is the customer.

Clerks should help each customer with their return. Have at least three conversations with different customers.

Customers should choose one item from **G** to return or exchange. Use one of the reasons you came up with. Have at least three conversations with different clerks.

For Sale!

GOAL ▶ Sell a product

A If you were going to sell some items you owned, what would they be? Make a list on a separate piece of paper.

B Read each of the ads below and think about these questions.

1. What is for sale?

2. How is the seller trying to convince you to buy?

3. Would you consider buying any of the items in the ads? Why?

Rare Red Dino 1973 Ferrari 246 GTS
This car, a sporty red convertible, will make you feel like royalty.
- Right-hand drive
- 50,000 miles before restoration
- 10,500 miles after restoration
- One owner
- Serious inquiries only

Save on gas!
Buy a bicycle! This bike, a fun means of transportation, will get you around in style.
- In great shape
- 6 months old
- $275
Reply to this ad to take it for a test ride.

C Study the chart.

Appositives		
Noun or Noun Phrase	**Appositive**	**Remainder of Sentence (Predicate)**
The ad,	**the one with all the great pictures,**	makes me want to buy those dishes.
That computer,	**the fastest machine in the store,**	sells for over $2,000.

Explanation:
- An appositive is a noun or noun phrase that renames another noun next to it in a sentence.
- The appositive adds extra descriptive detail, explains, or identifies something about the noun. If the appositive is taken out of the sentence, the sentence still makes sense.
- An appositive can come before or after the noun phrase it is modifying.

Example: *A helpful gift, money is always appreciated by a newly married couple.*

Note: Appositives are usually set off by commas.

D Find and underline the appositive in both ads in **B**.

E Complete each of the statements with an appositive.

1. Her dress, _____a really fancy gown_____, got the attention of every customer in the room.

2. That used car, _____, will probably be for sale for quite a while.

3. Used pots and pans, _____, are hard to sell without the matching lids.

4. Two round-trip plane tickets, _____, can be used to travel anywhere in the United States.

5. The smartphone, _____, has 64 GB of storage.

6. Those leather shoes, _____, have many more years of walking in them.

7. This restaurant, _____, will make you money as soon as you open the doors.

8. That set of suitcases, _____, will carry enough clothing and accessories for two weeks of traveling.

9. Her website, _____, is an online store with tons of gently worn clothes for sale.

F If you wanted to buy these things, where would you look?

1. car: _____

2. shoes: _____

3. music: _____

4. furniture: _____

G Imagine that you are going to sell something. Answer the questions and then discuss your ideas with a partner.

1. What would you sell? _____

2. What would you say to make your product sound appealing? _____

_____

3. How much would you sell it for? _____

4. Where would you place your ad? _____

5. How would you want people to contact you? _____

H Write three statements with appositives that you could use in your advertisement.

1. _____

2. _____

3. _____

I On a separate piece of paper, write an ad to sell your product. Find an attractive photo to draw attention to your ad.

J Share your ad with your classmates. See if you can find anyone who would buy what you are selling.

Life ONLINE There are many apps you can use to buy used items or sell some of your own items. You just need to download the app, set up an account, and then you can browse ads or take a picture and sell your own item. Some apps are used for selling anything, from a car to a treadmill to a bookshelf while other apps are more specific, just for buying / selling clothing, for example.

Explore the Workforce

GOAL ▶ Explore the role of a customer service representative

A **Read the situations and the questions. Discuss your answers with a partner.**

1. You order a fan online and when you receive it, it doesn't work. What do you do?

2. Your electricity bill is much higher than the previous month. What do you do?

3. You get in a minor car accident, and you need to report it to the insurance company. What do you do?

If you have good listening and communication skills and you like to talk on the phone or text, a *customer service representative* could be a great job for you. Most customer service representatives only have a high school diploma and almost all companies will train you on the job.

B **Look at the list of tasks. What kind of company do you think a person who does this works at? Write your ideas. Try to come up with a different company for each task.**

CUSTOMER SERVICE TASKS

1. Talk with customers on the phone to take an order.

   clothing store, furniture store
   _____

2. Determine charges for services and arrange for billing.

   _____

3. Review insurance policy terms to decide if a particular loss is covered by insurance.

   _____

4. Prepare invoices for a customer's return.

   _____

5. Record details of a customer complaint, as well as actions taken.

   _____

6. Prepare change of address records, or issue service discontinuance orders.

   _____

C INTERPRET Customer service representatives shared details about their daily activities. Read the information and make sentences with a partner.

EXAMPLE: *Thirty percent of customer service reps have limited freedom to make decisions.*

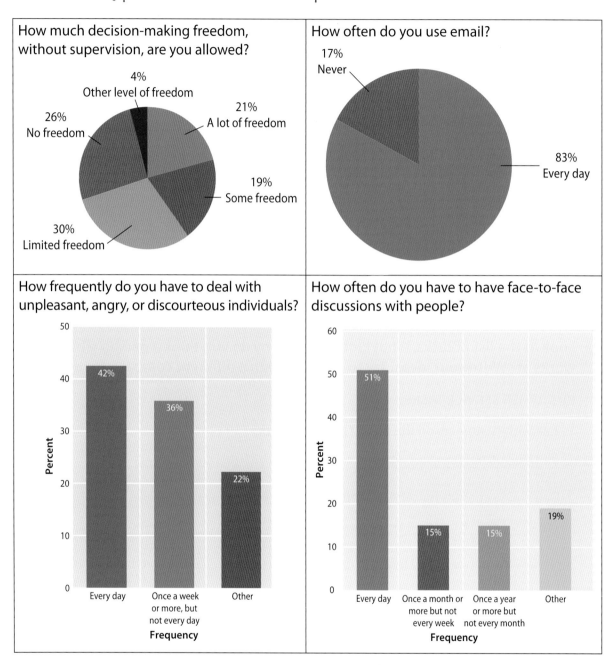

D **What makes a good customer service representative? Read the text and make a list of the skills needed. Then mark each one that you are good at.** 🎧

In order to be a customer service representative, you must be able to listen to and understand information. This is called oral comprehension. You also must be able to communicate information and ideas when speaking so people can understand you. This is called oral expression. In addition, you need to make sure that you are speaking clearly so that you can be understood, which is called speech clarity. As a customer service representative, you will be listening to people with all different accents and voice registers. So you will need to be able to identify and understand the speech of other people. This is called speech recognition.

Every day, you will get calls from people who have a problem. You need to have problem sensitivity, which means understanding when something is wrong or likely to go wrong, in other words, being sensitive to the person on the other end of the line. Sometimes you will need to write a report about a conversation, so your written expression is important, communicating information and ideas in writing so others will understand. Also, you need to be able to understand what you are reading when reading other people's written memos or documents, which is written comprehension.

There are two types of reasoning involved with being a customer service representative: deductive reasoning and inductive reasoning. Deductive reasoning means that you can take general rules and apply them to a specific problem to come up with an answer that makes sense. On the other hand, inductive reasoning means that you can combine different pieces of information to form a general rule or conclusion. I'm sure that you already have many of these skills in your toolbox. And the good news is that you will get better at all of them the more time you spend on the job.

1. _____
2. _____
3. _____
4. _____
5. _____
6. _____
7. _____
8. _____
9. _____

E **REFLECT Tell your partner what you are good at.**

EXAMPLE: I am *good at listening and understanding when people are talking.* (oral comprehension)

Review

A Imagine that you are going to buy a used car. Write four questions you would ask car sellers.

1. _____

2. _____

3. _____

4. _____

B Ask your classmates the questions you wrote in **A**. In your notebook, write some of their responses. When your classmates ask you their questions, you can talk about your own car or a car you are familiar with.

C Imagine that you are going to buy a product online. In your notebook, write a short paragraph about the steps you will need to take to buy the product.

D Write a conversation between a salesperson and a customer for one of the items in the catalog in Lesson 2.

Salesperson: _____

Customer: _____

Salesperson: _____

Customer: _____

Salesperson: _____

Customer: _____

E Read this warranty and choose *T* (true) or *F* (false).

DELTA warrants this product against defects in material and workmanship under normal use and service for one year from the original purchase date. DELTA will repair or replace the defective product covered by this warranty. Sales receipt is required as evidence of the date of purchase and for any warranty service. This warranty is only valid if the product has been handled and used as described in the instructions accompanying this warranty. This warranty does not cover any damage due to accident, misuse, abuse, or negligence.

Learner Log	I can do product research.	I can purchase goods and services by phone and online.	I can interpret product guarantees and warranties.
	Yes No Maybe	Yes No Maybe	Yes No Maybe

176   UNIT 6

1. This warranty is good for two years.   T   F

2. DELTA will replace your product if it gets stolen.   T   F

3. You need your receipt to get service under this warranty.   T   F

4. This warranty covers product defects.   T   F

F **Read the return policy and the situations. In pairs, practice asking questions about returning items. One student is the customer and one is the clerk. Then switch roles.**

Valid photo ID required for all returns (except for credit card purchases), exchanges, and to receive and redeem store credit. With a receipt, a full refund in the original form of payment, except payments made with checks, will be issued for new and unread books and unopened products within four days. For merchandise purchased with a check, a store credit will be issued within seven days of purchase. Without an original receipt, a store credit issued by mail will be offered at the lowest selling price. With a receipt, returns of new and unread books and unopened music from our website can be made for store credit. Textbooks after 14 days or without a receipt are not returnable. Used books are not returnable.

1. return books with the original receipt   2. return textbooks after three weeks

3. return two calendars without a receipt   4. exchange unopened products

G **Write appositives to complete each statement.**

1. This pre-owned car, _____, has been thoroughly inspected and is in tip-top shape.

2. This laptop computer, _____, still has a two-year warranty.

3. Two theater tickets, _____, can be used any weeknight in the month of August.

4. The bicycle, _____, has barely been ridden.

H **Using one of the statements in G, write an ad for the product on a separate piece of paper. Include an appositive in the ad.**

Learner Log   I can return a product.   I can sell a product.
                    Yes   No   Maybe   Yes   No   Maybe

Vocabulary Review

A **Use each word in a sentence.**

1. allege: _____

2. guarantee: _____

3. quality: _____

4. convince: _____

5. malfunction: _____

6. policy: _____

B **Share the sentences you wrote in A with a partner. Write your partner's best sentence.**

_____

C **Match each word to its synonym.**

Word	Synonym
_____ 1. return	a. claim
_____ 2. refund	b. promise
_____ 3. model	c. match
_____ 4. guarantee	d. replace
_____ 5. exchange	e. reimburse
_____ 6. convince	f. persuade
_____ 7. conform	g. type
_____ 8. allege	h. take back

Create an Online Store

SOFT SKILL ▶ Collaboration

1. Form a team of four or five students. Choose positions for each member of your team.

Position	Job Description	Student Name
Student 1: Project Leader	Check that everyone speaks English. Check that everyone participates.	
Student 2: Secretary	Take notes on your team's ideas.	
Student 3: Designer	Design layout of catalog or web page.	
Student 4: Director	Assign each team member one part of presentation. Organize presentation so that individual parts create a unified whole.	
Student 5: Assistant	Help secretary and designer with their work.	

2. Decide the name of your store and what you will sell. Select a variety of items to sell.

3. Create the following items for your store: catalog or web page, the store's return policy, a warranty / guarantee policy.

4. Prepare a poster that contains all of the information in Steps 2 and 3.

5. Present your store's catalog pages or web page to the class.

COLLABORATION

Brainstorm Ideas

1. Have everyone write down their ideas on a piece of paper and then share.
2. Go around the group and share one by one.
3. Discuss the different ideas.

Digital Literacy Tip: Use a shared document to brainstorm. If everyone has access, you can type your ideas and everyone will be able to see them.

Reading Challenge

A With a partner, come up with definitions for the following phrases. If you need to use a dictionary, write the definitions in your own words.

eco-friendly: _____

sustainable fashion: _____

inclusive sizing: _____

zero waste: _____

carbon footprint: _____

B **PREDICT** Based on the phrases in **A**, what do you think the reading is going to be about?

_____

C Read *Eco-Friendly Jeans*. Underline the phrases you defined in **A**.

D Complete the following statements with a number.

1. It takes _____ gallons of water for this company to make a pair of jeans.

2. It takes _____ gallons of water to make a traditional pair of jeans.

3. The apparel and footwear industries account for over _____ of global climate impact.

4. A pair of jeans from this company costs less than _____.

5. This company treats and recycles _____ of the water they use.

E Based on what you read about Warp and Weft, do you agree that individual companies can make a difference to the future of the planet? Why or why not?

_____

_____

_____

_____

F If you could talk to Sarah, what are three questions you would like to ask her?

1. _____

2. _____

3. _____

Eco-Friendly Jeans

Warp and Weft CEO and founder, Sarah Ahmed, has one mission: to produce and sell the best sustainable denim. This New Yorker's eco-friendly fashion brand launched in 2017. She believes that people should be able to buy a pair of high-quality, stretch jeans without harming the environment. She also asserts that sustainable fashion can be affordable for everyone. All of
5 Warp and Weft products cost less than $100 and their sizing is inclusive.

Sarah believes in more than making a profit. If she is making products to sell, she wants to come as close to zero waste as possible. That's why her company manufactures some of the most eco-friendly denim around, saving over 572 million gallons of water. According to Warp and Weft's website, "A traditional pair of jeans takes 1,500 gallons of water to make, but a pair
10 of Warps requires less than 10. Beyond that, we treat and recycle 98% of the water we use. We also skip the environmentally-harmful bleaching process by opting for cutting-edge Dry Ozone technology, making us fully compliant with International Social and Environmental & Quality Standards."

Unfortunately, the apparel and footwear industries account for more than 8% of global
15 climate impact. In fact, textile waste has become a huge problem around the world. This photo is an example of the devastating effects of fast fashion on the planet. Tons of discarded clothing have turned the Atacama Desert into one of the world's largest textile dumps. One of the problems with fast fashion (getting fashionable clothing to consumers as quickly as possible) is that it has to be shipped by air. Warp and Weft uses a more sustainable transportation method:
20 they ship by boat.

To ensure that the clothing you are buying is eco-friendly and sustainable, look for products made from upcycled materials such as plastic, cotton, fibers, and old denim. Also, see if the products are made with minimal water consumption. Sustainability is an ongoing process. If you can, support companies who are using the latest technology, pushing for zero waste and
25 trying to minimize their carbon footprint.

Textile pollution in the
Atacama Desert, Chile

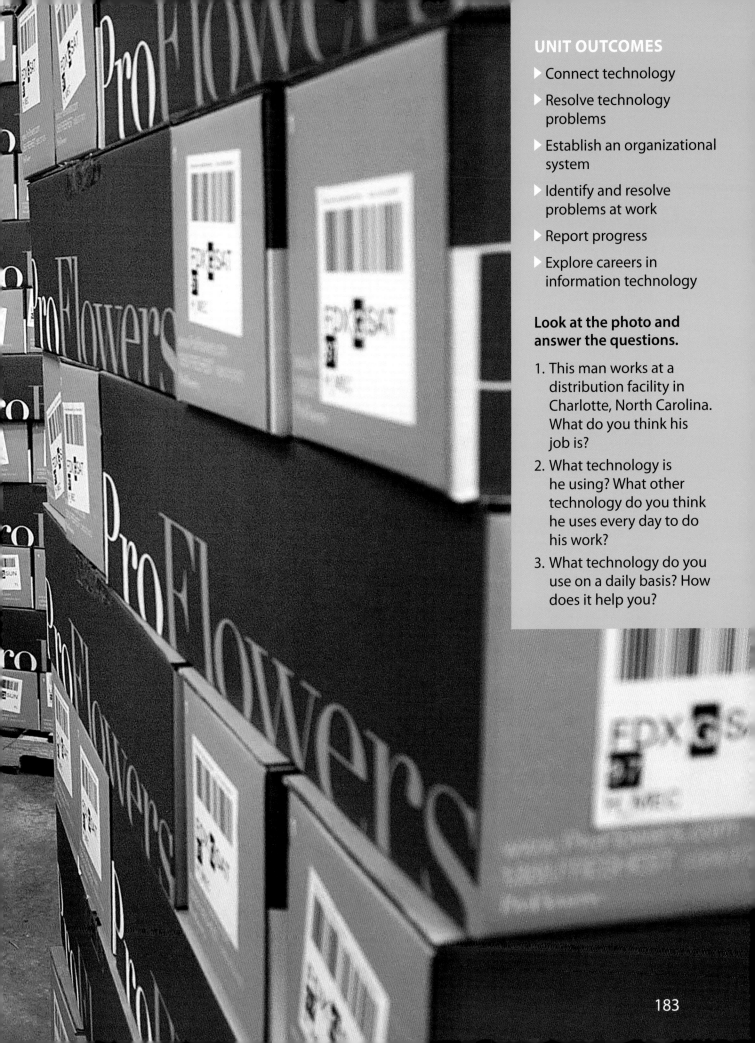

▶ Connect technology

▶ Resolve technology problems

▶ Establish an organizational system

▶ Identify and resolve problems at work

▶ Report progress

▶ Explore careers in information technology

Look at the photo and answer the questions.

1. This man works at a distribution facility in Charlotte, North Carolina. What do you think his job is?

2. What technology is he using? What other technology do you think he uses every day to do his work?

3. What technology do you use on a daily basis? How does it help you?

Vocabulary Builder

A Use these terms to label each item you might find in an office. Under each item, write a brief description of its purpose.

card reader	~~laptop~~	printer	ring light	tablet
handheld scanner	point of sale (POS) system	projector	security camera	

1.

laptop: process
information, create reports,
and do online research

2.

_____
_____
_____

3.

_____
_____
_____

4.

_____
_____
_____

5.

_____
_____
_____

6.

_____
_____
_____

7.

_____
_____
_____

8.

_____
_____
_____

9.

_____
_____
_____

B Draw pictures for these terms. Use a dictionary to look up any words you don't know, but remember to look for the definition that is related to technology.

headset	portable charger	HDMI port	ear buds

C Write a definition for each term.

1. troubleshoot: _____

2. paper jam: _____

3. scan: _____

D Look at the verbs in the table. Find the nouns and adjectives in the verbs' word families.

Verb	Noun	Adjective
accommodate		
avoid		
collaborate		
compete		
compromise		
motivate		
resolve		

How Do You Connect It?

GOAL ▶ Connect technology

A Read the instructions for connecting your computer to a printer.

1. After you install and set up the proper software on your computer or device, make sure your printer is plugged in and turned on.

2. Find the document from your computer or phone that you want to print.

3. To print from your phone, make sure the Bluetooth is turned on. To print from your computer, make sure you are connected to wifi.

4. Click the print button and select the printer.

B **SUMMARIZE** Reread the instructions in **A**. Then, in your own words, tell a partner how to connect and print from a phone or computer. (If you have a printer in your classroom, you can try to connect and print from a phone or laptop.)

C **Connecting to a Bluetooth speaker is like connecting a printer. Number the pictures to match them with the instructions.**

1. Charge the Bluetooth speaker by plugging it in.

2. Turn on the Bluetooth speaker.

3. Turn on the Bluetooth on your phone.

4. In the Bluetooth setting on your phone, select the name of the speaker. (It should say "Connected to XYZ speaker.")

5. Troubleshoot: If the speaker doesn't connect, push the pairing button on the speaker.

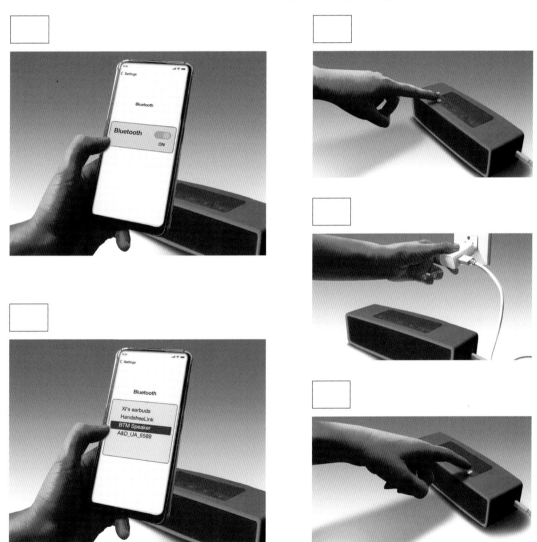

D **What are some other technology items that you can connect your phone to? What other technology items can you connect a Bluetooth speaker to? Make two lists on a separate piece of paper.**

I can connect my phone to…
I can connect a Bluetooth speaker to…

E Read about barcode scanners and answer the questions.

A barcode scanner is an optical device that can read and translate the series of lines and numbers on a product. It tells the computer what the item is and how much it costs. The scanner scans the barcode's black and white stripes by illuminating the code with a red light and the decoder interprets that signal, validates the barcode, and converts it into text.

Employees use barcodes when looking for information about products and processing purchases, but these days many stores have scanners you can use by yourself.

Here are some tips for using scanners:

- If you are using a handheld scanner to check the price, put the product's barcode near the scanner and press the button. You will get the cost of the product and it will also tell you if it's on sale.
- If you are using a barcode scanner at checkout (connected to a point of sale or POS system), put the product near the scanner with the barcode facing down. There will be a beep to let you know the bar code has been scanned and the price added to the POS system.
- If you're buying loose items that need to be counted or weighed, you'll need to know the item number. Sometimes there will be a small sticker on the item with a barcode or you can do a search in the POS system. Once the POS system knows what item you have, it will ask you to type in how many items you have or to put your items on the machine to be weighed.

1. What is a barcode? _____

2. What does a barcode scanner do? _____

_____

3. How do you know that a barcode has been scanned? _____

4. Explain what to do if the item doesn't have a barcode on it.

_____

_____

_____

_____

F GENERATE Look back at the list of technology items at the beginning of the unit. Choose one item that you are familiar with and write a list of instructions with illustrations. Review your instructions with a partner. Can your partner follow the instructions easily? Is the sequence of your instructions correct?

Troubleshooting

GOAL ▶ Resolve technology problems

A Think of some problems you have had in the past with technology. In a small group, discuss what the problems were and how you fixed them.

B Carla is having trouble with her printer. No paper comes out when she tries to print. Read what she found online.

Search Online	Suggestions
printer paper jam	• Clear jam by following instructions on printer screen. • Make sure the printer can handle the paper weight you are using.
printer paper stuck together	• Don't put too much paper in the printer tray. • Take the paper out, fan the pages, and put them back in. **Note:** Humidity can cause pages to stick together.
paper won't go through printer	• Remove any obstructions from inside the printer. • Open printer and look for obstructions.
document won't print	• Make sure both devices are connected (by Bluetooth or wifi). • Make sure printer is on.

C Answer the questions based on the troubleshooting guide in **B**.

1. What should you do if the document won't print?

_____

2. What causes pages to stick together? _____

3. What should you do if the paper won't feed through the printer? _____

_____

4. What should you do if there is a paper jam? _____

_____

D Read Carla's problem in **B** again. Write three suggestions you might give her.

1. _____

2. _____

3. _____

E Listen to the conversations between employees at different companies. Write the technology type, the problems, and suggestions for fixing them in the table. 🎧

Technology	Problem	Suggestions
		1. 2.
		1.
		1. 2. 3.
		1. 2. 3.

F Using the information you wrote in **E**, role-play the conversations with a partner. Take turns being the person with the problem.

G Maya has to take photos for her job as a home appraiser. She is having trouble with her phone. Match each problem to its solution. Some problems may have more than one solution.

_____ 1. Battery is losing its charge quickly.

_____ 2. Storage is full.

_____ 3. Camera app is frozen.

_____ 4. Camera app won't open.

a. Close other apps not being used.

b. Close out of app and restart.

c. Delete photos / videos.

d. Plug in a portable battery.

e. Restart phone.

f. Store photos / videos in the cloud.

H **SEQUENCE** Troubleshooting is a critical skill for Information Technology (IT) professionals. Sometimes, it is as simple as making sure the technology is plugged in or just restarting it. But that's not always the case. There are six steps IT professionals use to solve technology problems. What do you think the order is? Number the steps from 1–6.

_____ Determine what caused the problem.

_____ Check that the solution solved the problem.

_____ Establish a plan of action to solve the problem.

_____ Document your findings, actions and outcomes.

_____ Implement your solution.

_____ Identify the problem.

I **Choose one of these problems. Then write the steps (1–6) you would follow to solve it.**

a. Your laptop screen is frozen.

b. A Bluetooth speaker won't connect to your phone.

c. Your tablet won't turn on.

d. An app won't open on your phone.

1. _____

2. _____

3. _____

4. _____

5. _____

6. _____

J **Share your troubleshooting list with a partner.**

Life ONLINE
There are thousands of resources online to help you troubleshoot just about every technology problem you can face. From problems installing a computer operating system or a new doorbell camera, to issues with home appliances, devices, or your car, you are sure to find a tutorial or instructions manual online. Your owner's manual should always be your first resource—you don't want to invalidate your warranty—but if you're struggling to know how to use a feature of your new washing machine, or you can't figure how to use of a power tool to complete a home project, you can find lots of help online.

Get Organized!

GOAL ▶ Establish an organizational system

A **CLASSIFY** One way of organizing things is by putting similar items in groups. How would you organize this supply closet? Discuss your solutions with your classmates.

B Write how you would reorganize the supply closet. Then, on a separate piece of paper, do a simple drawing of the closet and show where you would keep each item.

_____

_____

_____

_____

_____

C Help Narit organize her files. Label the file *P* if it goes in the *Purchase Orders* folder. Label it *B* if it goes in the *Bank Statements* folder. Label it *I* if it goes in the *Invoices* folder. Label it *R* if it goes in the *Returns* folder. Compare your work with a partner.

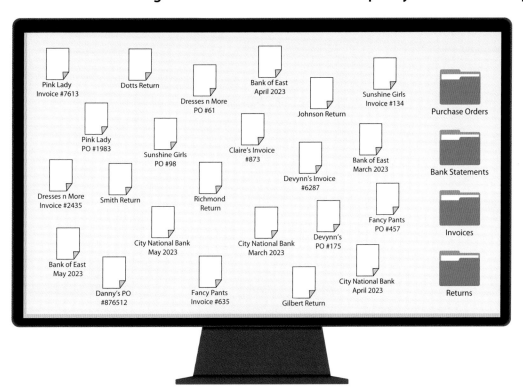

D On a computer, you can have a folder within a folder (a *subfolder*). You can also organize things in different ways. Answer the questions.

1. Which folder in **E** could have more than one subfolder folder? _____

2. What are the two different ways you could organize the subfolders?

    a. _____

    b. _____

E Take the documents from the *Invoices* folder and write them in order by invoice number.

1. _____   2. _____

3. _____   4. _____

5. _____   6. _____

F Narit decided to organize the invoices and purchase orders using the folders *Invoices* and *Purchase Orders*. What is another way she could have organized these files? Discuss with a partner.

G Dave works for a satellite TV company and uses his phone for work. He can never find anything when he needs it. Look at his phone screens. Make a list of at least five different folders he could use to organize his apps. Label each folder. Then write the apps that go in each folder. Some apps won't fit into a folder.

Health				
B-fit				

H Share your work with a partner. Did you group your apps in the same way? Did you come up with similar folder names?

I Think of something at your workplace or in your home that needs to be organized. On a separate piece of paper, answer the questions.

1. What needs to be organized?

2. Why? What is the problem?

3. How would you plan to organize it?

What's the Problem?

GOAL ▶ Identify and resolve problems at work

A **Answer the following questions with a partner.**

1. What is *conflict resolution*?

2. Where are some places that conflicts might occur?

3. Who are some people that you might have conflicts with?

4. Think about the ways you handle conflicts with people. What would you say your personal style of behavior is when speaking to people in a conflict?

B **PREDICT** **Read the questions before each section of the article. Think about them as you read.** 🎧

1. What are the three benefits of resolving conflict?

2. What can happen if conflict is not handled effectively?

3. What are the five steps to resolving a conflict?

Conflict Resolution: Resolving Conflict Rationally and Effectively

In many cases, conflict in the workplace just seems to be a fact of life. The good news is that by resolving conflict successfully, you can solve many of the problems that it has brought to the surface, as well as get benefits that you might not at first expect.

1. **Increased understanding:** The discussion needed to resolve conflict expands people's awareness of the situation, giving them an insight into how they can achieve their own goals without undermining those of other people.

2. **Increased group cohesion:** When conflict is resolved effectively, team members can develop stronger mutual respect and a renewed faith in their ability to work together.

3. **Improved self-knowledge:** Conflict pushes individuals to examine their goals in close detail, helping them understand the things that are most important to them, sharpening their focus, and enhancing their effectiveness.

However, if conflict is not handled effectively, the results can be damaging. Conflicting goals can quickly turn into personal dislike. Teamwork breaks down. Talent is wasted as people disengage from their work. And it's easy to end up in a vicious downward spiral of negativity and recrimination.

C **Choose the best answer according to what you read in B.**

1. What is NOT one of the benefits of resolving conflict?
    a. learning more about yourself
    b. a negative workplace
    c. better understanding of one another
    d. stronger respect for team members

2. What can happen if conflict is not handled effectively?
    a. You can lose your job.
    b. The company could file for bankruptcy.
    c. People will disengage and not want to work together.
    d. You may get a promotion.

D **It can be challenging to talk through a conflict. Read the phrases and choose the ones you are familiar with. Discuss with your teacher when these phrases are used.**

☐ Let's take a break and come back to this when we've thought about it and cooled down a bit.

☐ Help me understand where you're coming from.

☐ Thank you for being honest with me.

☐ How can I support you?

☐ What I heard you say is . . . Did I get that right?

☐ I agree with you about . . .

☐ Let's work on this problem together.

☐ I see how I've been a part of the problem.

☐ I'm sorry.

☐ What do you suggest we do about this?

☐ Let's see how we can prevent this from happening in the future.

☐ I hear your point of view, but I have a different way of thinking about it.

☐ Agree to disagree?

E Read the text.

Using the Tool: *A Conflict-Resolution Process*

Step One: Set the scene.

Make sure that people understand that the conflict may be a mutual problem, which may be best resolved through discussion and negotiation rather than through raw aggression.

Step Two: Gather information.

Here, you are trying to get to the underlying interests, needs, and concerns of the other people involved. Ask for the other people's viewpoints and confirm that you respect their opinions and need their cooperation to solve the problem.

Step Three: Agree on the problem.

This sounds like an obvious step, but often different underlying needs, interests, and goals can cause people to perceive problems very differently. You'll need to agree on the problems that you are trying to solve before you can find a mutually acceptable solution.

Step Four: Brainstorm possible solutions.

If everyone is going to feel satisfied with the resolution, it will help if everyone has had fair input into generating solutions. Brainstorm possible solutions and be open to all ideas, including ones you never considered before.

Step Five: Negotiate a solution.

By this stage, the conflict may be resolved—both sides may better understand the position of the other, and a mutually satisfactory solution may be clear to all.

F With a partner, write a conversation using one of these scenarios (a–e). Try to use the five steps to conflict resolution from **E** as well as some of the phrases from **D**.

a. You are working in a team to create a product design. One of the team members isn't contributing. Instead she is on her phone, taking long breaks and coming in late.

b. The manager of a clothing boutique has started a friendly competition between employees, offering a $1,000 bonus to whoever sells the most this week. Two employees have started acting dishonestly to steal customers from one another.

c. Elias is an accountant for a software production company. He needs the sales figures at the end of each month to create his reports. Dalia always gives him her figures late, which affects his report.

d. Your company is relocating to a new office, at least 45 minutes away from the current one. Several employees are resistant to this change.

e. Andre is speaking in a meeting when his co-worker, Selena, interrupts him. In the next meeting, he notices that Selena interrupts him a few more times, and he cannot fully express his ideas.

G Practice your conversation and present it to the class.

What Did You Do?

GOAL ▶ Report progress

A Maria's supervisor asked her to write a progress report about a long-term project she is working on. Read the guidelines he gave her. 🎧

Progress Report Guidelines

You write a progress report to inform a supervisor, associate, or customer about progress you've made on a project over a certain period of time. In the progress report, you explain all of the following:

- what the project is
- how much of the work is complete
- which part of the work is currently in progress
- what work remains to be done
- what problems or unexpected issues have arisen

B **ANALYZE** Read part of Maria's report. Is she following the guidelines so far?

To: Henry Kim, Human Resources Director
From: Maria Avalos
Date: April 14th
Subject: Program for Employee Training

It seems that many problems have arisen from the employees working such long hours and not being able to communicate effectively with one another. It was proposed that I put together a training program for our employees on conflict resolution.

So far, I have been conducting research on whether it is better to bring in an outside training organization or do the training ourselves. I have concluded that it would be more cost-effective for us to do the training ourselves. So, I am currently working on putting together a training manual that can be used for the conflict-resolution training. I foresee that it will take me another two weeks to complete the manual. Once it has been completed, we will need to choose several people to conduct the training and train them to be effective leaders.

C Is anything missing from Maria's report? If so, write what is missing.

_____

_____

D Study the chart.

Noun Clauses as Objects		
Subject + Verb	**Noun Clause**	**Explanation**
I did	*what* I was asked.	• A noun clause starts with a question word or *that* and is followed by a subject and verb. • In these examples, the noun clause is the object of the sentence.
She knows	*how* the computer works.	
They decided	*where* the location would be.	
My boss asked	*who* would be best for the job.	
I hope	*that* they work as a team.	

E Complete each of the sentences with an appropriate noun clause from the list. More than one noun clause may be appropriate.

how the filing system worked	~~what she told me to~~
how to complete the progress report	where the files were stored
that they would be promoted	who got to receive the training
that we knew what we were doing	who wanted to be the team leader

1. I did _what she told me to_____.

2. She found _____.

3. The supervisor asked _____.

4. He explained _____.

5. Our team showed _____.

6. Sari asked _____.

7. Jared and Giulia hoped _____.

8. The representative chose _____.

F Complete each sentence with a noun clause of your own.

1. I asked _____.

2. I hoped _____.

3. I decided _____.

4. I explained _____.

G Maria reports that she has encountered problems. Read the problems and write a paragraph from Maria's perspective. Include what she might suggest as solutions.

- The employees do not want this training.

- None of the supervisors who could be trainers want to lead the training.

_____

_____

_____

_____

_____

_____

H With the information given, write a progress report. Use the guidelines in **A** and the format of Maria's report in **B**. Using the examples in **D** and **E**, include noun clauses in your report.

Project: Change the way scheduling of staff is handled.

Work completed: Servers and bartenders have been interviewed.

Currently in progress: Interviewing the kitchen staff.

To do: Take information from interviews and come up with a better way to handle scheduling in the future.

Problems: Last-minute shift-switching without manager approval; some shifts are too short.

_____

_____

_____

_____

_____

_____

_____

_____

_____

_____

LESSON
6

Explore the Workforce

GOAL ▶ Explore careers in information technology

A **Information Technology (IT) is one of the most popular career fields. What do you think IT professionals do? Brainstorm a list of jobs or tasks.**

IT professionals…

repair computers	

B **What education do you think is required for careers in IT? Discuss with a partner. Then look at the bar graph and answer the questions on a separate piece of paper.**

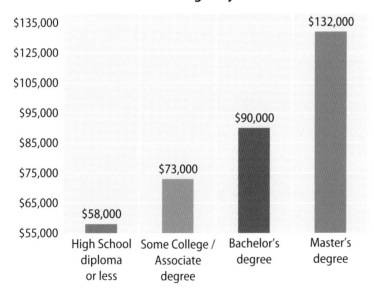

IT Professional Wages by Education

(Data source: bls.gov)

1. Do you need a college degree to work as an IT professional?

2. What is the difference in pay between people with a high school diploma and people with some college?

3. Is there a big difference in pay between a Bachelor's degree and a Master's degree?

4. Based on the education and pay, would it interest you to become an IT professional? Why?

C This chart gives some information on different IT jobs. Write a title for each column.

Computer and Information Research Scientist	design innovative uses for new and existing technology	Master's	$131,490
Computer Network Architect	design and build data communication networks, including local area networks (LANs), wide area networks (WANs), and intranets	Bachelor's	$120,520
Computer Programmer	modify and test code and scripts that allow computer software and applications to function properly	Bachelor's	$93,000
Computer Support Specialist	maintain computer networks and provide technical support to computer users	Some college/ Associate	$57,910
Computer Systems Analyst	study an organization's current computer systems and design ways to improve efficiency	Bachelor's	$99,270
Digital Designer	develop, create, and test website or interface layout, functions, and navigation for usability	Bachelor's	$78,300
Database Administrator	create or organize systems to store and secure data	Bachelor's	$101,000
Information Security Analyst	plan and carry out security measures to protect an organization's computer networks and systems	Bachelor's	$102,600
Network Systems Administrator	responsible for the day-to-day operation of computer networks	Bachelor's	$80,600
Software Developer	design computer applications or programs	Bachelor's	$109,020
Web Developer	create and maintain websites	Bachelor's	$78,300

D Practice asking and answering questions with a partner. Use information from the chart in C.

A: What does a computer support specialist do?

B: A computer support specialist maintains computer networks and provides technical support.

A: How much does a web developer make?

B: About $78,000.

A: Do you need a Master's degree to be a digital designer?

B: No, you just need a Bachelor's degree.

E Practice making true and false statements with a partner. Use information from the chart in **D.**

A: You need a Master's degree to be a web developer.

B: That's not true.

F Read the job post and find this information: job title, location, salary, education required, experience required, skills required, job responsibilities.

WE ARE HIRING!

Computer Programmer

Highlight Technology

Baltimore, MD

Salary Range

$66K–$89K

Apply on employer site

Responsibilities

- ✓ Perform daily morning review of network systems to ensure proper operation
- ✓ Respond to customer problems / needs as part of local helpdesk staff
- ✓ Troubleshoot network, computer, and device issues
- ✓ Work on development tasks as needed

Qualifications

- ✓ Associate degree. Computer programming related education, training, or certification is preferred.
- ✓ 5 years of experience
- ✓ Expertise in programming procedures and working with complex programs

Required skills:

- ✓ C#
- ✓ ASP.NET MVC
- ✓ TSQL
- ✓ Microsoft SQL Server
- ✓ JavaScript
- ✓ jQuery
- ✓ HTML
- ✓ CSS

G Choose one of the jobs in **C.** Find an online job post. Write these details on a separate piece of paper.

Job title

Location

Salary

Education required

Experience required

Required skills

Job responsibilities

Review

A **Read the instructions for connecting a Bluetooth headset to your computer. Then answer the questions.**

Step 1: Make sure your Bluetooth headset is in "discoverable mode." To do this, push the button on the right headphone to enter "pairing mode."

Step 2: Click on the *Start* menu on your PC and go to your PC settings.

Step 3: From the settings, click on *Devices*.

Step 4: Enable Bluetooth by clicking on the toggle and selecting *Add Bluetooth or Other Device*.

Step 5: In the pop-up window, click *Bluetooth*. This will scan all nearby Bluetooth devices.

Step 6: Once your headphones show up in the list, select them and click *Connect*.

1. How do you put your headset into discoverable mode?

_____

2. Where do you find *Devices* on your computer?

_____

3. How do you enable Bluetooth?

_____

4. What do you click once your headphones show up in the list?

_____

B **Read the troubleshooting tips for a Bluetooth headset. Then choose the best answer.**

What to do if your headphones won't connect:

1. Check that they are fully charged.

2. Check the Bluetooth set up. It may need to be reset.

3. Make sure your headphones aren't connected to another device.

1. If your headphones won't connect,

   a. reset them.

   b. make sure they are fully charged.

   c. disconnect them from all other devices.

   d. all of the above

2. If your headphones won't connect, why should you check the Bluetooth set up?

   a. They may be connected to another device.

   b. They may need to be reset.

   c. You may need to buy a new pair.

   d. The batteries may need charging.

Learner Log	I can connect technology.			I can resolve technology problems.		
	Yes	No	Maybe	Yes	No	Maybe

C These files need to be organized in folders. Create and write a folder name in each box. Then match the files to the correct folder.

Order #13245.docx

Order #7754.docx

Printer Manual.pdf

Tax Return 2021.pdf

Order #16278.docx

Bluetooth Speaker Manual.pdf

Order #7826.docx

POS System Manual.pdf

Tax Return 2022.pdf

Camera Manual.pdf

Digital Assistant Manual.pdf

Tax Return 2023.pdf

Tax Return 2020.pdf

D Answer the following questions about the conflict-resolution articles in Lesson 4.

1. What are three benefits of resolving conflict?

   a. _____

   b. _____

   c. _____

2. What are the five steps for resolving conflict?

   a. _____   b. _____

   c. _____   d. _____

   e. _____

E Write the five things a progress report should include.

   1. _____   2. _____

   3. _____   4. _____

   5. _____

Learner Log	I can establish an organizational system.	I can identify and resolve problems at work.	I can report progress.
	Yes No Maybe	Yes No Maybe	Yes No Maybe

Vocabulary Review

A Put each term in the correct column according to its part of speech: *noun, verb,* or *adjective.*

click	cost-effective	force	organize	reorganize
conflict	effective	long-term	paper jam	satisfactory
connect	files	mutual	power supply	settings

Noun

1. _____
2. _____
3. _____
4. _____
5. _____

Verb

1. _____
2. _____
3. _____
4. _____
5. _____

Adjective

1. _____
2. _____
3. _____
4. _____
5. _____

B Use words from **A** to complete the sentences. Not all the words are used.

1. Did you get a chance to put the _____ in alphabetical order?

2. The computer wasn't working because the _____ wasn't plugged in.

3. _____ on the settings from the *Start* menu.

4. It doesn't seem _____ to have so many computers running at the same time. That wastes a lot of energy.

5. Tim, can you _____ these files? They seem to have gotten out of order.

6. If you _____ the paper into the feeder, it will probably cause a _____.

7. The project isn't going well. It seems like the members of her team are having a _____.

8. We need a(n) _____ solution to this disorganized supply closet.

9. I hope we can come up with a _____ solution.

10. I wonder why the Bluetooth speaker won't _____ ?

Looking for a Job

SOFT SKILL ▶ Active Listening

A Units 6 and 7 have covered a variety of workplaces. In a group, brainstorm workplaces and different jobs you might find in them.

Office

B Mark the jobs in **A** that you think earn the most money.

C Research jobs online and see if you can add to your lists in **A**.

D Choose two jobs that seem the most interesting to you and fill in the table.

Job Title	Salary	Training / Qualifications Required

ACTIVE LISTENING:
Polite disagreements

Polite interactions are key to the success of any team. If disagreements arise, let others express their thoughts fully without interrupting them. Then confirm that you understand what was said by repeating it or asking clarifying questions. Allow others to elaborate on their thoughts. It is important to not try to force our ideas on others. The goal of a brainstorming session is to quickly gather as many ideas as possible. Not all ideas will be good. The team as a whole has to decide which ideas are the best ones and how to refine them.

Reading Challenge

A Think about the workplace 20 years ago compared to today. How do you think it was different? Brainstorm in a small group.

B **PREDICT** You will see these phrases in the reading. Guess their meanings.

no match: _____

the new norm: _____

hybrid model: _____

healthy spaces: _____

strikes a balance: _____

on the rise: _____

C Read *The New Workplace*. Underline the phrases from **B**.

D Look at the underlined phrases. Does the meaning you wrote in **B** fit the meaning in the reading? Choose three of the phrases and write your own sentences with them.

1. _____

2. _____

3. _____

E **SUMMARIZE** Write a one-paragraph summary of the new workplace, according to the reading.

_____

_____

_____

_____

F At the end of the article, the author says, "Hopefully, this new model is here to stay." Do you agree or disagree? Why?

_____

_____

_____

_____

The New Workplace 🎧

The Covid pandemic showed us how much we value human interaction. Although working from home was a necessary solution during that time, some people think that online meetings are no match for a shared workplace experience and human connection. Others agree that physical presence in an office space is not necessary. Many good things came out of the
5   pandemic, one of them being how we view the workplace.

The new workplace is mobile. Employers and employees have realized that many people can be just as productive, if not more, at home. And now that the office is open again, many people are still at home. Research has shown that people who spend at least some of their workweek out of the office have higher workplace satisfaction, job commitment and engagement and are
10   more innovative. A hybrid model has become the new norm, where employees spend some time at the office and work from home for the other part of their workweek.

The new workplace also has more focus on health and wellness. Before 2020, workers' desires for a healthy workplace were not being met. During the pandemic, people began to prioritize well-being, learning to take care of themselves and keep themselves healthy. As they came back
15   to the workplace, they wanted this focus on health to continue. Therefore, employers are feeling pressure to prioritize physical and psychological well-being by offering flexibility and healthy spaces at work, whether it be outdoor workspaces or fitness opportunities during breaks.

The new workplace strikes a balance between open spaces and privacy. The open space concept, where employees work collaboratively instead of having their own private offices, has
20   been on the rise for years. Although open spaces have been associated with higher performance and a greater work experience, the noise, lack of privacy, and the inability to remain focused are detrimental to this concept. It is key for companies to work on a better space allocation that still allows for collaboration but also gives employees the option of private spaces to work in.

We have learned that working completely from home or spending 40 hours in the office
25   does not necessarily bring out the best in everyone. Employees have realized what they want and need, and employers have learned that achieving workplace balance is key to productivity and healthy, happy employees. Hopefully, this new model is here to stay.

A man works from home enjoying the company of his dog.

8 Civic Responsibility

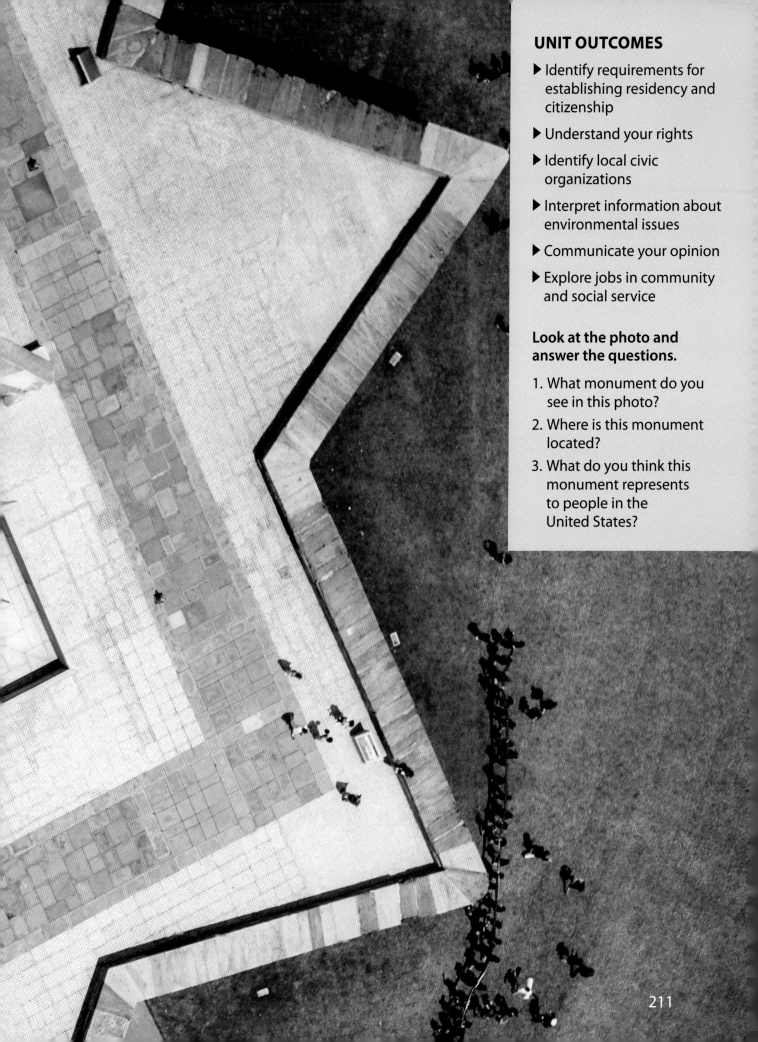

UNIT OUTCOMES

▶ Identify requirements for establishing residency and citizenship

▶ Understand your rights

▶ Identify local civic organizations

▶ Interpret information about environmental issues

▶ Communicate your opinion

▶ Explore jobs in community and social service

Look at the photo and answer the questions.

1. What monument do you see in this photo?
2. Where is this monument located?
3. What do you think this monument represents to people in the United States?

211

Vocabulary Builder

A INFER Read each sentence and infer the meaning of the italicized word and identify its part of speech. Then look each word up in a dictionary.

1. The judge gave an *impartial* verdict that did not favor either side.

   Part of speech: _____ Meaning: _____

   _____

   Dictionary definition: _____

2. There are so many *commuters* on the roads today that there is always a lot of pollution and noise.

   Part of speech: _____ Meaning: _____

   _____

   Dictionary definition: _____

3. We all must *conserve* energy so that we can protect the environment for our kids.

   Part of speech: _____ Meaning: _____

   _____

   Dictionary definition: _____

4. During the war, many *refugees* went to safer countries to live better lives.

   Part of speech: _____ Meaning: _____

   _____

   Dictionary definition: _____

5. She runs a *charitable* organization that gives food to homeless people.

   Part of speech: _____ Meaning: _____

   _____

   Dictionary definition: _____

B Each sentence in **A** reflects the topic of a lesson in this unit. Look at the sentences and guess what each lesson will be about.

1. _____

2. _____

3. _____

4. _____

5. _____

C **CLASSIFY** Look at the list of terms. Categorize each term by writing it under the correct lesson title.

bear arms	eligible	protect	slavery
believe	immigrant	punishment	social welfare
capital crime	naturalization	refugee	status
civic	opinion	resource	
conserve	peaceably assemble	reusable	

Identify requirements for establishing residency and citizenship	Understand your rights	Identify local civic organizations	Interpret information about environmental issues	Communicate your opinion

D Write your own sentence for each of the words.

1. naturalization: _____

2. punishment: _____

3. civic: _____

4. reusable: _____

5. resource: _____

Investigating Citizenship

LESSON **1**

GOAL ▶ Identify requirements for establishing residency and citizenship

A How can an immigrant become a permanent resident of the United States? Make a list of your ideas.

1. _____

2. _____

3. _____

4. _____

B **PREDICT** Several students in Mrs. Morgan's class want to become permanent residents of the United States. Read about each nonresident and decide if you think he or she is eligible to become a permanent resident. Write *yes* or *no*.

1. Hanh has been living in the US since 2000. She recently became engaged to a US citizen. Is she eligible? _____

2. Sadiq is a refugee from Iraq who has been here for six months. Is he eligible? _____

3. Ella is 35, married, and her mother just became a permanent resident. Is she eligible? _____

4. Phillipe has lived in the US since 1975. Is he eligible?

_____

5. Enrique and his wife are doctors from Guatemala. Are they eligible?

_____

C Some of the most common Green Card (permanent resident) eligibility categories are Family, Employment, Refugee / Asylee, and Registry. Read the following information that can be found on the US Citizens and Immigration Services Website. 🎧

Family: You may be eligible if you are . . .
- the spouse of a US citizen
- an unmarried child under the age of 21 of a US citizen
- the parent of a US citizen who is at least 21 years old
- a family member of a US citizen, meaning you are the:
  - unmarried son or daughter of a US citizen and you are 21 years old or older
  - married son or daughter of a US citizen
  - brother or sister of a US citizen who is at least 21 years old
- a family member of a lawful permanent resident, meaning you are the:
  - spouse of a lawful permanent resident
  - unmarried child under the age of 21 of a lawful permanent resident
  - unmarried son or daughter of a lawful permanent resident 21 years old or older
- a person admitted to the US as a fiancé(e) of a US citizen (K-1 nonimmigrant)
- a person admitted to the US as the child of a fiancé(e) of a US citizen (K-2 nonimmigrant)
- a widow or widower of a US citizen and you were married to your US citizen spouse at the time your spouse died

Employment: You may be eligible if you . . .
- have extraordinary ability in the sciences, arts, education, business or athletics, or
- are an outstanding professor or researcher, or
- are a multinational manager or executive who meets certain criteria, or
- are a member of a profession that requires an advanced degree, or
- are a skilled worker (meaning your job requires a minimum of 2 years training or work experience), or
- are a professional (meaning your job requires at least a US Bachelor's degree or a foreign equivalent and you are a member of the profession), or
- are an unskilled worker (meaning you will perform unskilled labor requiring less than 2 years training or experience)

Refugee / Asylee: You may be eligible if you . . .
- were granted asylum status at least one year ago
- were admitted as a refugee at least one year ago

Registry: You may be eligible if you . . .
- have resided continuously in the US since before Jan. 1, 1972.

D Look at the nonresidents in **B**. Do you need to change some of your answers? Discuss each situation with a partner and decide what specific details would make each person eligible for permanent resident status.

E Listen to a talk about the requirements for becoming a citizen. Fill in the missing words and phrases.

      United States citizenship carries many (1) _____ with it. The decision to become a US citizen is a very important one. Being granted US citizenship is known as (2) _____. In most cases, a person who wants to naturalize must first be a (3) _____ resident. By becoming a US citizen, you gain many rights that permanent residents or others do not have, including the (4) _____. To be eligible for naturalization, you must first meet certain (5) _____ set by US law.

      What are the basic requirements to apply for naturalization? Generally, to be eligible for naturalization you must:

- Be at least (6) _____ old;
- Show you have been a lawfully admitted permanent resident of the United States for at least (7) _____;
- Demonstrate (8) _____ in the United States for at least five years immediately before the date you file Form N-400;
- Show you have been physically present in the United States for at least (9) _____ out of the (10) _____ immediately before the date you file Form N-400;
- Show you have lived for at least (11) _____ in a state or USCIS district having jurisdiction over your place of residence. (If you are a student and are financially dependent on your parents, you may apply for naturalization where you (12) _____ or where your family (13) _____.);
- Show that you are a person of (14) _____ and have been a person of good moral character for at least five years;
- Demonstrate an attachment to the principles and ideals of the (15) _____;
- Be able to read, write, and speak (16) _____;
- Have knowledge and understanding of the fundamentals of the (17) _____, and of the principles and form of (18) _____, of the United States, (civics);
- Take an Oath of (19) _____ to the United States.

F Look at the words and phrases you wrote in E. Do you understand the meanings? Discuss with a partner.

G ANALYZE How many requirements are there to be able to apply for naturalization? Which ones do you think may be difficult to prove? Discuss in a group.

H Do you know people who have become permanent residents or citizens? In your notebook, write a short paragraph about someone you know and their process.

Rights

GOAL ▶ Understand your rights

A **SUMMARIZE** In 1791, the Bill of Rights was added to the United States Constitution. Read and paraphrase the first 10 amendments. 🎧

Amendment I Congress shall make no law respecting an establishment of religion, or prohibiting the free exercise thereof; or abridging the freedom of speech, or of the press; or the right of the people peaceably to assemble, and to petition the government for a redress of grievances.

Amendment II A well regulated militia, being necessary to the security of a free state, the right of the people to keep and bear arms, shall not be infringed.

Amendment III No soldier shall, in time of peace be quartered in any house without the consent of the owner, nor in time of war, but in a manner to be prescribed by law.

Amendment IV The right of the people to be secure in their persons, houses, papers, and effects, against unreasonable searches and seizures, shall not be violated, and no warrants shall issue, but upon probable cause, supported by oath or affirmation, and particularly describing the place to be searched, and the persons or things to be seized.

Amendment V No person shall be held to answer for a capital, or otherwise infamous crime, unless on a presentment or indictment of a grand jury, except in cases arising in the land or naval forces, or in the militia, when in actual service in time of war or public danger; nor shall any person be subject for the same offense to be twice put in jeopardy of life or limb; nor shall be compelled in any criminal case to be a witness against himself, nor be deprived of life, liberty, or property without due process of law; nor shall private property be taken for public use without just compensation.

Amendment VI In all criminal prosecutions, the accused shall enjoy the right to a speedy and public trial, by an impartial jury of the state and district wherein the crime shall have been committed, which district shall have been previously ascertained by law, and to be informed of the nature and cause of the accusation; to be confronted with the witnesses against him; to have compulsory process for obtaining witnesses in his favor, and to have the assistance of counsel for his defense.

Amendment VII In suits at common law, where the value in controversy shall exceed twenty dollars, the right of trial by jury shall be preserved, and no fact tried by a jury shall be otherwise reexamined in any court of the United States than according to the rules of the common law.

Amendment VIII Excessive bail shall not be required, nor excessive fines imposed, nor cruel and unusual punishments inflicted.

Amendment IX The enumeration in the Constitution of certain rights shall not be construed to deny or disparage others retained by the people.

Amendment X The powers not delegated to the United States by the Constitution, nor prohibited by it to the states, are reserved to the states respectively, or to the people.

B **Match each amendment with the right it guarantees.**

_____ 1. The first amendment guarantees

_____ 2. The second amendment guarantees

_____ 3. The third amendment guarantees

_____ 4. The fourth amendment guarantees

_____ 5. The fifth amendment guarantees

_____ 6. The sixth amendment guarantees

_____ 7. The seventh amendment guarantees

_____ 8. The eighth amendment guarantees

_____ 9. The ninth amendment guarantees

_____ 10. The tenth amendment guarantees

a. a speedy and public trial by an impartial jury.

b. the right to be charged by a grand jury if accused of a serious crime.

c. that people have other rights not listed in the Bill of Rights.

d. freedom of religion.

e. that people, homes, and belongings are protected from unreasonable search and seizure.

f. the right to keep and bear arms.

g. that people have all the rights not given to the government by the Constitution.

h. that government cannot force people to house soldiers during times of peace.

i. a trial by jury in civil cases (disputes between private parties or between the government and a private party).

j. that no excessive bail or fines will be imposed and that punishment will not be cruel and unusual.

C **Read each situation. Then decide which amendment describes your rights. Write the amendment numbers on the lines.**

1. Your friend is Jewish and celebrates Hanukkah, but you are Christian and don't celebrate it. _____

2. You have a registered gun in your house, locked up in a safe. _____

3. The police can't come into your home without a warrant. _____

4. If you are convicted of a crime, your punishment will not be cruel. _____

5. If you are accused of a crime, you will get a fair trial. _____

D INTERPRET There is currently a total of 27 amendments to the Constitution. Read four of the amendments and answer the questions that follow. 🎧

Amendment XIII (1865)

Neither slavery nor involuntary servitude, except as a punishment for crime whereof the party shall have been duly convicted, shall exist within the United States or any place subject to their jurisdiction.

Amendment XV (1870)

The right of citizens of the United States to vote shall not be denied or abridged by the United States or by any state on account of race, color, or previous condition of servitude.

Amendment XIX (1920)

The right of citizens of the United States to vote shall not be denied or abridged by the United States or by any state on account of sex.

Amendment XXVI (1971)

The right of citizens of the United States who are 18 years of age or older to vote shall not be denied or abridged by the United States or any state on account of age.

1. What does the thirteenth amendment guarantee? _____

2. The fifteenth, nineteenth, and twenty-sixth amendments are all about the same right.

   What is it? _____

3. How are these three amendments different?_____

   _____

   _____

4. In the original Constitution, why do you think so many groups of people were not given the

   right to vote? _____

   _____

E ANALYZE Discuss the following in a small group.

Do any of the rights identified in this lesson affect your life? Which ones? In what ways?

F Create a Bill of Rights for your classroom or school.

Getting Involved

GOAL ▶ Identify local civic organizations

A Read about civic organizations. 🎧

A civic organization is a group of people who come together for educational or charitable purposes, including the promotion of community welfare. The money generated by these groups is devoted exclusively to charitable, educational, recreational, or social welfare purposes.

B Read about a civic organization. 🎧

Big Brothers Big Sisters of Eastern Massachusetts

History

The Big Brothers Big Sisters organization of eastern Massachusetts (BBBSEM) was started in 1949 by volunteers who wanted to create an organization for boys without fathers in Boston, Massachusetts. It started with the simple, but now proven successful, idea to match 10 boys with 10 adult volunteers who were able to offer them help and guidance. Now the group serves around 5,000 youths annually and has made 20,000 matches over the last seven decades.

Fundraising

A. Winter: The "Big Night" is an evening of live music at a local music venue. It is also an auction.

B. Spring: A Casino night is held in April. Guests dress in their finest for an evening of socializing, networking, and table games. Winnings go to the organization.

The ticket includes food, dancing, casino chips, and the opportunity to bid for grand prizes.

C. Summer: The Golf Classic is the organization's keystone fundraiser. Over 400 golfers get together in June for a golf tournament at a golf club. Local and national companies sponsor the event.

Community Service

BBBSEM has other programs such as the Campus-Based program, which brings kids who live in places without convenient access to public transportation to college campuses to match them with college students who they meet with on weekends.

Social

"Bigs" and "littles" are encouraged to spend time together doing activities from bowling and bike riding to attending local concerts together.

C Answer these questions with a partner. Share your answers in a small group.

1. What makes BBBSEM a civic organization?
2. What civic organizations are there in your community?

D **Read about these organizations and answer the questions.**

 **Friends of
the Library**

Mission: To provide materials, support summer reading programs, provide cultural and literacy events for the community and fund training for the library staff.
Membership: Senior $10, Individual $20, Student $15, Family $25

 **American
Hiking Society**

Purpose: To enjoy the outdoors and also help raise public awareness of issues that face the present-day outdoors, including public lands and trails.
Members: Anyone who enjoys hiking
Annual Dues: $125–$1,000

 **Garden Club
of America**

Mission: To stimulate the knowledge and love of gardening, to share the advantages of association by means of educational meetings, conferences, correspondence, and publications, and to restore, improve, and protect the quality of the environment through educational programs and action in the fields of conservation and civic improvement.
Members: Anyone who enjoys gardening
Donation: varies

 **Rotary Club**

Mission: To provide service to others, promote integrity, and advance world understanding, goodwill, and peace through fellowship of business, professional, and community leaders.
Members: Membership in a Rotary club is by invitation only. We want to make sure you join a club that best fits your passion and perspective. We can connect you with a club that's right for you and make it easy to get involved and on your way to membership immediately.
Initiation Fee: $100
Annual Dues: $300

1. Which group would you join if you liked nature? _____

2. Which group do you have to be invited to join? _____

_____

3. Which group has the highest dues? _____

   The lowest? _____

4. Which groups help their members? _____

5. Which groups help people in the community? _____

_____

6. If you could join one group, which one would it be? Why? _____

_____

E Some of the students from Mrs. Morgan's class want to create a civic organization. They have come together because they have common interests. Read about the students and then come up with ideas for their organization. 🎧

Hanh, Sadiq, Ella, Phillipe, and Enrique have just found out that many students at their school can't afford to buy books. There are over 100 students a year who attend class without textbooks. Hanh, Sadiq, Ella, Phillipe, and Enrique have one thing in common— they are all very creative. Sadiq takes beautiful photographs, Hanh and Ella both knit and can make anything from hats to sweaters and blankets, Phillipe is an accomplished musician and songwriter, and Enrique paints oil paintings of flowers and animals.

Name of civic organization: _____

Mission: _____

_____

Members: _____

_____

Annual dues: _____

_____

Special events: _____

_____

F **CREATE** Follow the directions and create a civic organization.

Step 1. Get together with a few students from your class and create a new civic organization. Complete the information about your organization.

Name of civic organization: _____

Mission: _____

_____

Members: _____

_____

Annual dues: _____

Special events: _____

_____

Step 2. Recruit members for your organization. You need at least ten members to be a true organization.

Saving the Environment

GOAL ▶ Interpret information about environmental issues

A Look at the list of ways to create less trash. Choose the ones you do.

☐ Buy items in bulk from loose bins when possible to reduce the packaging wasted.

☐ Avoid products with several layers of packaging when only one is sufficient.

☐ Buy products that you can reuse.

☐ Maintain and repair durable products instead of buying new ones.

☐ Check reports for products that are easily repaired and have low breakdown rates.

☐ Reuse items like bags and containers when possible.

☐ Use cloth napkins instead of paper ones.

☐ Use reusable plates and utensils instead of disposable ones.

☐ Use reusable containers to store food instead of aluminum foil and cling wrap.

☐ Shop with a canvas bag instead of using paper and plastic bags.

☐ Buy rechargeable batteries for devices used frequently.

☐ Reuse packaging cartons and shipping materials. Old newspapers make great packaging material.

☐ Buy used furniture—there is a surplus of it, and it is much cheaper than new furniture.

B Interview a partner to find out how they conserve energy at home. Mark what they do.

☐ Clean or replace air filters on your air-conditioning unit at least once a month.

☐ Lower the thermostat on your water heater to 120°F.

☐ Wrap your water heater in an insulated blanket.

☐ Turn down or shut off your water heater when you will be away for extended periods.

☐ Turn off unneeded lights even when leaving a room for a short time.

☐ Set your refrigerator temperature at 36 to 38°F and your freezer at 0 to 5°F.

☐ When using an oven, minimize door opening while it is in use.

☐ Clean the lint filter in your dryer after every load so that it uses less energy.

☐ Unplug seldom-used appliances.

☐ Use a microwave whenever you can instead of a conventional oven or stove.

☐ Wash clothes with warm or cold water instead of hot.

☐ Turn off lights, computers, and other appliances when not in use.

☐ Use compact fluorescent lightbulbs to save money and energy.

☐ Keep your thermostat at 68°F in winter and 78°F in summer.

☐ Use cold water instead of warm or hot water when possible.

☐ Connect your outdoor lights to a timer.

C A civic organization whose mission is to support healthier air quality has put together several action items that they would like to see accomplished in their communities. Read their plan for carpooling. 🎧

Carpooling: What is it?

Carpooling is an arrangement by a group of commuters to ride together from home or a prearranged meeting place in a van or a car to their destinations in a single round trip, with the driver as a fellow commuter. Carpools usually consist of individuals who live near each other and are employees of the same company, or are employees of different companies located only a short distance apart, and who have the same work hours. The great advantage of carpools is that they reduce vehicle trips and vehicle miles traveled, and they therefore reduce auto emissions that result in poor air quality.

Shared Impact and Benefits

- Carpooling reduces overall auto emissions by reducing vehicle miles traveled, and by doing so, improves air quality.
- Peak-hour traffic congestion and resulting gasoline consumption are reduced. In 2020, traffic congestion caused 1.7 billion gallons of fuel to be wasted.
- Employers can offer employees a value-added benefit and take a tax write-off.
- Eight of ten US workers believe commuter benefits are valuable to employees.
- Furthermore, employers that pay for employee parking costs can save money.
- Carpool participants save money by sharing commuting costs.
- Carpool riders have less stressful commutes to work. Employers will also have more productive employees with higher morale.

Costs

Usually carpoolers share the costs of gasoline, maintenance, and / or leasing the vehicle. An electric / hybrid vehicle would be optimum.

How long does this take to implement?

A carpooling program can be implemented within a few months. Once the program is established, individual pools can be set up in less than a few weeks.

The Bottom Line

Carpooling commuters get to work in a way that reduces air pollution and traffic congestion, saves employers and employees money, reduces the environmental impacts associated with driving single-passenger vehicles, reduces parking space demand and expenses, and relieves commuter stress.

Who needs to be involved?

- Governing board and / or management (to endorse a carpool policy and support a program that provides incentives for employees who participate in a carpool)
- Businesses and their human resource or fiscal office staff
- Transit providers and / or private carpool leasing companies
- Private parking deck and lot owners
- Employees willing to start up their own carpool

D With a partner, choose one of the following three environmental topics. Make a list of programs that might work to improve the environment in your community.

air quality

water resources

sustainable development

Topic: _____

Possible programs: _____

_____

_____

_____

E Find another pair of students who chose the same topic as you. Work together and share your ideas. Then choose one program to develop. Think about and decide on these items.

Topic: _____

Name of program: _____

Brief description of how the program works: _____

_____

_____

_____

Impact on and benefit to the environment: _____

_____

_____

Length of time to implement: _____

Cost: _____

People involved: _____

Expressing Yourself

GOAL ▶ Communicate your opinion

A **BRAINSTORM** Everyone has an opinion when it comes to the environment. In a small group, brainstorm some *yes* and *no* opinions for each of these suggestions.

EXAMPLE: People should not be permitted to buy large cars that create a lot of pollution.

Yes: *If everyone bought smaller cars, pollution would be significantly reduced.*

No: *Many people need large cars for their families. Large cars are safer. They hold more people and more groceries.*

1. Our city should require all new car purchases to be electric or hybrid.

Yes	**No**
a. _____	a. _____
b. _____	b. _____
c. _____	c. _____

2. Everyone should take their own recyclable items to a recycling center.

Yes	**No**
a. _____	a. _____
b. _____	b. _____
c. _____	c. _____

3. Each home should only be allowed to use a certain amount of water each month.

Yes	**No**
a. _____	a. _____
b. _____	b. _____
c. _____	c. _____

B Practice communicating your opinion to a partner. Use these phrases.

I agree.	I believe …	I disagree.	I think …	In my opinion, …

EXAMPLE: **Student A:** *I think our city should build more carpool lanes.*

Student B: *I disagree. In my opinion, it is a waste of money because it won't make more people carpool.*

C Read the paragraph that Ella wrote communicating her opinion on the environment.

Our Most Precious Resource

There are many things we should do to protect our environment, but I think one of the most important things we can do is to conserve water. Why? Water is our most precious resource. I believe this for many reasons. One reason is that the human body is made up of 75% water. We can only live for about three days without water; therefore, we need to drink water to survive. Another reason that water is so important is that we need it to clean. We need water to clean our bodies, wash our dishes, flush our toilets, and launder our clothes. Can you imagine not being able to do any of these things? Still another reason is that plants and trees need water to grow and survive. Without plants and trees, humans wouldn't survive because plants give off the oxygen we need in order to breathe. For these reasons, I believe that we need to conserve our most precious resource—water.

D Answer the questions about the sentence types in Ella's paragraph.

1. What is Ella's topic sentence?

   _____

2. What is Ella's concluding sentence?

   _____

3. Ella gives three reasons to support her main idea. For each idea, she gives a supporting detail. What are her reasons and details?

   a. Reason: _____

      Detail: _____

   b. Reason: _____

      Detail: _____

   c. Reason: _____

      Detail: _____

E ANALYZE Study these transitional expressions with your teacher. Which ones did Ella use in her paragraph?

Transitional Expressions		
One reason	The *first* reason	*Some* people
⇓	⇓	⇓
Another reason	The *second* reason	*Other* people
⇓	⇓	⇓
Still another reason	The *third* reason	*Still* others
• Use these phrases to connect your ideas.		
• Choose the set of phrases that works best for your topic.		
• Don't shift back and forth among sets of phrases.		

F Choose an environmental issue you feel strongly about. Brainstorm ways to resolve the issue by creating a cluster diagram on a separate piece of paper.

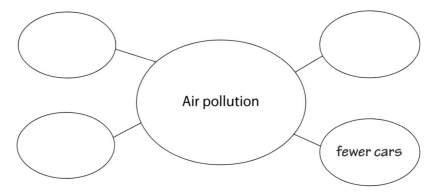

G Look at the cluster diagram in **F**. Write complete sentences explaining the ways in which your chosen environmental issue can be resolved.

Reason 1: _____

_____

Reason 2: _____

_____

Reason 3: _____

_____

H On a separate piece of paper, write a paragraph communicating your opinion about the environmental issue you chose in **F**.

Explore the Workforce

GOAL ▶ Explore jobs in community and social service

A What is a counselor? _____

B There are different types of counselors. Can you name a few?

1. _____

2. _____

3. _____

C Read the graph and the text about community and social service job growth. 🎧

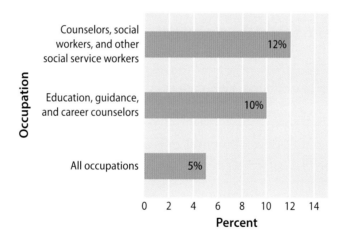

Job Growth from 2021-2031

Counselors fit into a larger group of occupations in the community and social service sector. Workers in these occupations promote wellness to help people cope with or overcome challenges. Overall employment in the community and social service sector is projected to grow 12 percent from 2021 to 2031. This is faster than the average for all occupations where the growth is only projected to be 5 percent. This increase should result in about 294,600 new jobs over the decade. There will also be a need to replace workers who leave their occupations permanently, adding to the job growth.

D Choose the correct answer.

1. The job growth of all occupations is increasing **faster / slower** than the job growth for social workers.

2. Employment in community and social services is projected to grow **more than / less than** 10 percent.

3. Job growth for school and career counselors is **less than / more than** the growth for other counselors and social workers.

E Talk with a partner and see if you know what each occupation is.

career counselor	rehabilitation counselor
community health worker	school counselor
health education specialist	social and human service assistant
marriage and family therapist	social worker
probation officer / correctional treatment specialist	substance abuse, behavioral disorder, and mental health counselor

F Complete each statement with the correct job title from **E**.

1. A _____ teaches people how to adopt healthy behaviors.

2. A _____ helps people choose a path to employment.

3. A _____ develops programs to teach people about conditions that affect well-being.

4. A _____ assists in the rehabilitation of law offenders who are in custody or on probation or parole.

5. A _____ helps people with physical, mental, developmental, or emotional disabilities live independently.

6. A _____ helps students develop academic and social skills.

7. A _____ advises people on various issues, such as those relating to alcoholism, addictions, or depression.

8. A _____ provides client services in a variety of fields, such as psychology, rehabilitation, and social work.

9. A _____ helps people prevent and cope with problems in their everyday lives.

10. A _____ helps people manage and overcome problems with their relationships.

G Mark each job in **E** that you have *never* heard of before.

H The professionals in this sector work with people of all ages. List the job titles in **E** under the appropriate age group. Some will fit under two or all three.

Children	Teenagers	Adults of All Ages

I REFLECT Mark the age group(s) you would be willing to work with.

J Work with a partner to complete each statement.

EXAMPLE: A rehabilitation counselor could help a person who *has a drug addiction*.

1. A family therapist works with teenagers who _____.

2. A career counselor helps people who _____.

3. A community health worker is giving a presentation on _____.

4. The social worker is helping that woman who _____.

K Choose one of the jobs that you marked in **H** that you would like to learn more about. Do an online search and gather this information:

Job title: _____

Salary range: _____

Education needed: _____

Skills required: _____

_____

_____

Job responsibilities: _____

_____

_____

_____

Review

A **List four ways a person can become a permanent resident of the United States.**

1. _____

2. _____

3. _____

4. _____

B **List four requirements for becoming a US citizen.**

1. _____

2. _____

3. _____

4. _____

C **Write the correct amendment number in front of each description.**

1. The _____ amendment is about the abolishment of slavery.

2. The _____ amendment is about the right for women to vote.

3. The _____ amendment is about the right to be charged by a grand jury if accused of a serious crime.

4. The _____ amendment is about protection from unreasonable search and seizure.

5. The _____ amendment is about cruel and unusual punishment.

6. The _____ amendment is about a speedy and public trial by an impartial jury.

7. The _____ amendment is about freedom of religion.

8. The _____ amendment is about the right to keep and bear arms.

9. The _____ amendment is about the right for people of all races to vote.

10. The _____ amendment is about protection from forced housing of soldiers.

Learner Log	I can identify requirements for establishing residency and citizenship. ☐ Yes ☐ No ☐ Maybe	I can understand my rights. ☐ Yes ☐ No ☐ Maybe

D Create a civic organization for the following group's problem.

A group of children who live in a shelter for homeless families goes to a nearby elementary school. However, the parents of the children don't have any money to buy the required school uniform—blue pants and a white shirt. The volunteers at the shelter want to find a way to raise money for these kids.

Name of organization: _____

Purpose: _____

Members: _____

Annual dues: _____

Special events: _____

E Work with a partner and list five ways you can help protect and preserve the environment.

1. _____

2. _____

3. _____

4. _____

5. _____

F Choose one of the ways you can help protect and preserve the environment in **E** and write a paragraph about why it is important.

_____

_____

_____

_____

_____

_____

_____

_____

_____

Learner Log	I can identify local civic organizations.	I can interpret information about environmental issues.	I can communicate my opinion.
	Yes No Maybe	Yes No Maybe	Yes No Maybe

Vocabulary Review

A Choose five words from the vocabulary list. Use each word in a meaningful sentence that reviews an important point or piece of information that you have learned in this unit.

bear arms	eligible	protect	slavery
believe	immigrant	punishment	social welfare
capital crime	naturalization	refugee	status
civic	opinion	resource	
conserve	peaceably assemble	reusable	

1. _____

2. _____

3. _____

4. _____

5. _____

B Use five different words from the list in **A** to write five different opinions you have.

1. _____

2. _____

3. _____

4. _____

5. _____

C Write the correct word from **A** in front of each definition.

1. _____ means resident foreigner.

2. _____ means having the right to do or be chosen for something.

3. _____ means a payment for doing something wrong.

4. _____ means useful things.

5. _____ means a legal condition.

Give an Opinion Speech

SOFT SKILL ▶ Presentation Skills

In this project, you will work individually to develop an opinion speech supported with details.

1. Look back at everything you have learned in this unit and choose one topic to give a speech about. Your speech should be persuasive. You should not just present facts without giving your opinion. However, you can support your opinion with facts. First, write one sentence that states your opinion.

   EXAMPLE:

   - *I think that someone should be able to become a citizen anytime he or she wants.*

   - *I don't think Americans should have the right to bear arms.*

   - *I think every citizen should have to be a part of a civic organization.*

2. Read your opinion out loud to the class.

3. Come up with reasons to support your opinion and write a speech. Prepare to speak for at least two minutes.

4. Practice your speech. Remember the following tips:

   - Enunciate (speak clearly).

   - Make eye contact with your audience.

   - Practice so you can recall your major points without notes.

   - Thank your audience for listening and / or for their time.

5. Give your two-minute opinion speech. At the end of your speech, ask your classmates if they have any questions.

PRESENTATION SKILLS
Peer feedback
Ask a partner to listen to your speech and give you feedback, not on the ideas but on the presentation. Are you speaking clearly? Are you making eye contact? Are you speaking slowly enough to be understood?

Reading Challenge

A Have you heard the phrase *the American dream*? Brainstorm what *the American dream* means to people.

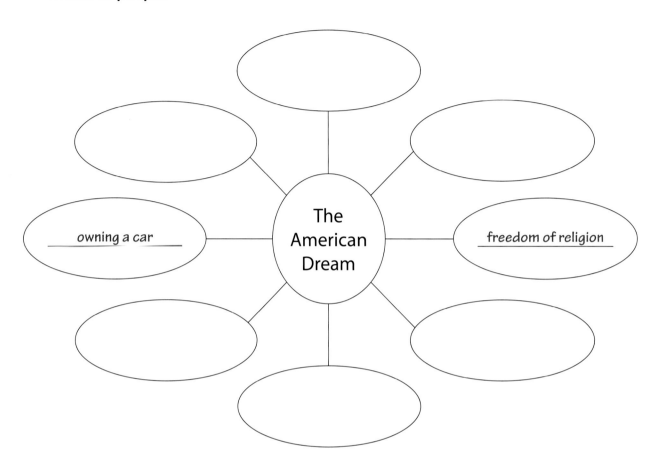

B Read *The American Dream*.

C Review the reading and complete the quotes.

1. Life should be better and richer and fuller for everyone, with opportunity for each

_____

2. . . . where they will not be judged by the color of their skin but by

_____

3. . . . an equal opportunity to achieve success and prosperity through

_____

D Next to each quote in **C**, write who said it or where it came from.

E Choose one of the quotes in **C**. In your notebook, explain what it means.

The American Dream 🎧

1   What is the American dream? Is it buying a home, finding a life partner and having two kids and a dog? Is it being able to live freely without religious persecution? Is it being able to find a job and move up the ladder to owning your own business? Traditionally, the American dream has meant upward social mobility and the financial ability to live a comfortable life. It's defined

5   by the Oxford American Dictionary as "the ideal that every citizen of the United States should have an equal opportunity to achieve success and prosperity through hard work, determination, and initiative." It is this dream that has brought so many immigrants to this country. The dream of having equal opportunity to work hard and succeed. The immigrant family in the photo had just passed the difficult examination to enter into the United States. For many immigrants being

10   allowed to come to the US is the first step to reaching the American dream.

But where did the phrase *the American dream* come from? The term *American dream* was actually coined by James Truslow Adams in 1931 in his book titled *Epic of America*. He described it as "that dream of a land in which life should be better and richer and fuller for everyone, with opportunity for each according to ability or achievement." It was again referred to 32 years

15   later by an American Baptist minister and activist, Martin Luther King Jr., in his famous "I Have A Dream" speech in 1963: *I still have a dream. It is a dream deeply rooted in the American dream. I have a dream that one day this nation will rise up and live out the true meaning of its creed: "We hold these truths to be self-evident, that all men are created equal…" I have a dream that my four little children will one day live in a nation where they will not be judged by the color of their skin but*

20   *by the content of their character.* Martin Luther King Jr.'s American dream goes hand in hand with Adams' definition which focuses on "everyone" and "opportunity for each." Both of these men believed the American dream was for anyone and everyone.

Every year, over one million immigrants come to the United States with a dream: they want access to the American dream. The American dream isn't universal. It means something

25   different to everyone. But the *idea* of the American dream *is* universal. People want to live in a place where they feel free to live the life they want; live the life they deserve. That freedom is the American dream.

An immigrant family looks at the New York City skyline while waiting for the ferry after passing the immigration examination.

Get The Facts Straight

What kind of source is it?

TODAY´S OPINION

Birds Aren´t Real

Dr. Ima Liar

Who is speaking?

What is the author's purpose?

How do they support their claims?

Before You Watch

A **Choose the places where you look for information online. Then share your answers with a partner.**

- ☐ blogs
- ☐ social media posts
- ☐ company websites
- ☐ news websites
- ☐ opinion articles and videos
- ☐ encyclopedias and reference sites

B **Read the words and phrases. Then complete the sentences.**

claim confirms exaggerate perspectives promotes red flag relevant reliable

1. A _____ is a sign that there might be a problem.

2. If an expert _____ a fact, they agree and say that it is true.

3. A person you can trust to tell you the truth is a _____ source.

4. When you tell someone that a thing is bigger or faster or funnier than it really is, you _____.

5. When a website _____ a product, they try to convince people to buy or use that product.

6. People with different _____ have different opinions or points of view about a topic.

7. When you _____ something, you say that it is true but you don't give any evidence.

8. A _____ study is clearly related to the idea you are learning about.

While You Watch

C Watch the video. Mark what the video says you should pay attention to in order to decide if information is reliable.

☐ 1. who the author is   ☐ 6. what other experts say

☐ 2. how long the website is   ☐ 7. number of likes or shares

☐ 3. related advertisements   ☐ 8. incomplete information

☐ 4. what sources are listed   ☐ 9. how you feel

☐ 5. website name   ☐ 10. print or online format

D Read the items and watch the video again. Match the questions to the answers.

_____ 1. What kind of source is it?   a. Other experts confirm their claims.

_____ 2. Who is talking?   b. an expert with relevant experience or a degree

_____ 3. What is the author's purpose?   c. calm and interested, not angry or upset

_____ 4. How do they support their claims?   d. to explain, inform, or share new research

_____ 5. What do other people say?   e. with links to recent studies and relevant data

_____ 6. How does it make me feel?   f. a newspaper, a government website, or
                                                  an academic study

After You Watch

E Read each sentence. Choose *T* (true) and *F* (false).

1. If a website is created by a company, it might promote that company's products.   T   F

2. Articles that make us feel strong emotions are usually the most reliable ones.   T   F

3. You should ignore any article labeled *Opinion*.   T   F

4. A fact-checking website can help you determine if a story is true.   T   F

5. You should never ignore articles with incorrect information or claims.   T   F

6. If an article claims something amazing is true and doesn't provide any data,   T   F
   that is a red flag.

F With a partner, write three tips from the video. Which one is most useful? Will you use any of these tips when you do research online? Are there other ways to make sure you are reading and sharing reliable information?

Life Skills Video Practice

UNIT 1   The Presentation is Due in Two Weeks

A   **BEFORE**   **Discuss the questions with a partner.**

1. Do you get nervous speaking in front of a crowd? Why or why not?

2. With a partner, write a list of things you think make a succesful presentation.

B   **WHILE**   **Watch the video and complete the parts of the conversation.**

Naomi: Come on, you guys. We have to do this (1) _____ in two weeks.

Hector: The assignment was to do a presentation on jobs and (2) _____.

Naomi: . . . if you take (3)_____ and write a (4) _____, then I'll make the (5) _____.

Mateo: That'll give me a week to (6) _____ my (7) _____.

C   **AFTER**   **Read the statements and choose the one that is false.**

1. Hector takes notes while they talk.

2. Hector needs a week to finish the report.

3. Naomi makes a pie chart to show the statistics.

UNIT 2   It's Called Identity Theft

A   **BEFORE**   **Discuss the questions with a partner.**

1. What are some examples of identity theft?

2. What can we do to avoid identity theft?

B   **WHILE**   **Watch the video and complete the parts of the conversation.**

Mateo: Wait a second. Where's my (1) _____ ? I can't find it.

Mr. Sanchez: Such as your driver's (2) _____ or social security (3) _____?

Naomi: You'd better notify the (4) _____ right away.

Mr. Sanchez: Then you should call the (5) _____ company right away.

C   **AFTER**   **Read the statements and write *True* or *False*.**

1. Mateo thinks he lost his wallet at work. _____

2. Someone took $500 out of Mateo's bank account. _____

3. Mr. Sanchez tells Mateo to file a police report. _____

4. Mr. Sanchez wlll call the credit card company. _____

UNIT 3   I Wish I Had A Car

A   BEFORE   Discuss the question with a partner.

1. What is different about driving in the United States and driving in the country you are from?

B   WHILE   Watch the video and complete the parts of the conversation.

Naomi: Convertibles get good (1) _____ .

Mateo: Who cares about (2) _____ or mileage?

Hector: Personally, I would rather have something more (3) _____ , like that pickup.

Hector: If you got a pickup, you would have lots of (4) _____ in the back.

C   AFTER   Write a number next to each quote to show the correct order.

a. _____ "The mileage on an SUV is terrible."

c. _____ "A pickup? Are you serious?"

b. _____ "I can't imagine what the insurance for a car like that would cost."

d. _____ "I've heard hybrids barely use any gas."

UNIT 4   I'll Have My Handyman Fix It

A   BEFORE   Discuss the questions with a partner.

1. Who do people call when something is broken in their house? Make a list.

2. Have you ever had to call someone to fix something in your home?

B   WHILE   Watch the video and complete the parts of the conversation.

Hector: Yeah, the ceiling is still (1) _____ even though the rain has stopped.

Landlord: I see. Has the water (2) _____ the floor?

Hector: But we can't keep emptying out this (3) _____ day and night.

Naomi: And we can't be (4) _____ for any damage if the water spills over.

C   AFTER   Choose the word that completes each sentence.

1. That **dripping** / **clicking** sound is driving me crazy!

2. I got your **phone** / **text** message this morning.

3. I think a pool of water may still be on the **ceiling** / **roof**.

4. And the damage to the **ceiling** / **floor** is getting worse.

5. The handyman will be here around **8** / **10** a.m.

UNIT 5   I Think I Might Have A Problem

A   BEFORE   Complete the tasks with a partner.

1. Write a list of six types of addiction.

2. Rank the addictions from your list from *most serious* to least serious.

B   WHILE   Watch the video and complete the parts of the conversation.

Hector: Can I tell you something? I used to have an (1) _____ too.

Naomi: You? (2) _____?

Hector: I used to be addicted to junk food. I ate it (3) _____, even when I wasn't hungry.

Naomi: You mean—you had an eating (4) _____?

C   AFTER   Choose the correct word to complete each sentence.

1. People who buy more things than they can afford are **careful shoppers** / **shopaholics**.

2. When people do things they don't want to do, they may have an **addiction** / **addition**.

3. In **support** / **supporting** groups, people share their experiences.

4. A **counselor** / **council worker** can also offer help and support.

UNIT 6   What Could Go Wrong?

A   BEFORE   Discuss the questions with a partner.

1. Which items do you usually buy online? Why?

2. Do you prefer to buy some items in a store? Why?

B   WHILE   Watch the video and complete the parts of the conversation.

Mr. Sanchez: Miriam, I think you forgot to check the (1) _____ of all these things.

Mrs. Sanchez: Oh, Victor, I think you're right. I just (2) _____ on the pictures without (3) _____ the sizes.

Mr. Sanchez: Now, do you see why I wanted to be (4) _____?

Mrs. Sanchez: Well, I learned my lesson. (5) _____ online isn't as easy as I thought. From now on, I will be more careful.

C   AFTER   In your notebook, write four steps to purchase objects online.

UNIT 7 You Seem to Be Doing A Very Good Job

A BEFORE Discuss the questions with a partner.

1. What do you think makes someone a good manager?

2. What do you think makes someone a good colleague?

B WHILE Watch the video and complete the parts of the conversation.

Mr. Patel: This stick on the side is called a (1) _____.

Hector: That's really cool. The (2) _____ is so clear, and it's really big.

Mr. Patel: And there are (3) _____ on both sides for things like charging the battery, inserting the flash memory card, etc.

Hector: That's great! This is a really useful little (4) _____.

C AFTER In your notebook, write the differences and similarities between Hector's PDA and a device you use every day.

UNIT 8 Mom, I'm So Proud of You

A BEFORE Discuss the questions with a partner.

1. What are some steps to becoming a US citizen?

2. What are some benefits of being a US citizen?

B WHILE Watch the video and complete the parts of the conversation.

Naomi: You mean you've kept your Turkish (1) _____ this whole time?

Mrs. Sanchez: Yes. I've been a legal permanent (2) _____ until now.

Naomi: What made you (3) _____ your mind?

Mrs. Sanchez: Well, now I have more time, and I've been thinking it's more important to get (4) _____.

C AFTER Write the steps that Mrs. Sanchez needs to follow to become a US citizen

_____

_____

_____

_____

Stand Out Vocabulary List

PRE-UNIT

cook
creative
dear
do crossword puzzles
do yoga
draw
emotional
hobbies
knit
lift weights
mental
paint
physical
play soccer
play video games
read
run
swim
take pictures
watch movies
write

UNIT 1

achieve
addiction counselor
alcohol and drug abuse
    counselor
anger management
    counselor
auditory
balance
be flexible
bodily
career development
    counselor
career path
computer programmer
domestic violence
    counselor
earning power
eating disorder counselor
educational attainment
elementary school
    counselor
evaluate
family counselor
financial
fun
goal setting
graphic designer
grief counselor
high school counselor

inspire
intelligence
interpersonal
intrapersonal
joy
juvenile justice counselor
kinesthetic
learning style
linguistic
logical
long-term
marriage counselor
mathematical
mental health counselor
monitor
motivate
motivation
multiple
musical
naturalistic
nutritional counselor
photographer
positive outlook
prioritize
pursue
registered nurse
rehabilitation counselor
relationship counselor
rhythmic
short-term
spatial
sports counselor
support
tactile
time with family
verbal
veteran's counselor
visual
vocational counselor

UNIT 2

accountant
actuary
bankruptcy
bargain
budget cut
buy in bulk
capital gains
certificate of deposit (CD)
collateral
commit fraud
convert
counterfeit

counterfeit checks
credit
credit analyst
credit card
current income
daunting
debt
delinquent accounts
dumpster diving
earnings
expense
false pretenses
financial
financial analyst
financial planner
fraud
inflation
investment
liquid
liquidate
mortgage
mutual funds
net appreciation
penalty
periodically
phishing
pretexting
profitable
property
purchasing power
real estate
rent
renter's insurance
risk
risky
savings account
skimming
stock trader
stocks
subscriptions
unauthorized transactions
value
vehicle
worth

UNIT 3

accident
air filter
alternator
auto body repair
    technician
auto designer
auto electrician

auto engineer
auto instructor
auto sales manager
battery
bodily injury
brake fluid reservoir
car detailer
car rental agent
car salesperson
change
check
children
choose
collision
commute
convertible
coolant reservoir
coverage
disc brake
distributor
electric vehicle (EV)
exhaust manifold
fatalities
fill
fill up
find
four-door sedan
fuel injection system
hybrid
imagine
incident
inspect
limits of liability
look at
make
mechanic
mileage
minivan
model
MPG
muffler
odometer
pedestrians
perform
pickup truck
police officer
policy
power steering reservoir
premium
process engineer
quality testing engineer
radiator
rear axle

rear suspension
red light
replace
school bus
seat belts
speed limit
sports car
sport utility vehicle (SUV)
station wagon
stop sign
timing belt
tire technician
top off
Tow truck driver
two-door coupe
uninsured motorist
unrestrained
van
vehicle inspector
VIN
water pump

UNIT 4

abandon
activate
architects
architectural / engineering
    managers
burglarize
burglary
civil engineers
compensate
construction / building
    inspectors
construction managers
crime
deductible
deteriorate
disturbance
drafters
dwelling
enticing
estimate
evident
exterior
get
grounds
have
help
housing
landscape architects
let
liability

litigate
make
possess
premises
premium
prevent
responsibility
responsible
right
seize
summon
surveying / mapping
    technicians
surveyors
terminate
theft
thief
urban / regional planners
vacate
weapons

UNIT 5

addiction
adhesive bandages
adhesive cloth tape
affect
antibiotic ointment
antiseptic wipes
aspirin
at risk
burn
carbon footprint
choking
cold compress
compress dressing
deductive reasoning
depressed
depression
detoxification
eco-friendly
emergency phone
    numbers
EMT
first-aid kit
head injury
hydrocortisone ointment
ice pack
impair
impairment
inclusive sizing
inductive reasoning
insurance
insure

insured
medical bill
meditate
meditation
mental health
open wound
out of shape
paramedic
physiological dependence
poisoning
prescription medication
process
process addiction
psychological
    dependence
responsible party
roller bandage
scissors
self-esteem
shock
sterile gauze pads
sterile gloves
substance addiction
survive
survivor
sustainable fashion
thermometer
tolerance
treat
treatment
tweezers
twelve-step program
uninsured
withdrawal
zero waste

UNIT 6

allege
conform
convince
customer service
customer service
    representative
exchange
fault
free of charge
guarantee
make
malfunction
model
order
policy
quality

receipt
refund
research
return
review
transaction
warranty

UNIT 7

accommodate
avoid
business telephone
cable
card reader
collaborate
compete
compromise
computer
computer and information
    research scientist
computer network
    architect
computer support
    specialist
computer systems analyst
cost-effective
database administrator
digital designer
effective
faded
fan
feed
feeder
files
force
handheld scanner
headphone
headset
information security
    analyst
long-term
motivate
network system
    administrator
obstructions
organize
paper jam
photocopier
point of sale (POS) system
port
power supply
printer
projector

reorganize
resolve
ring light
security camera
software developer
splotchy
tablet
toner
web developer

UNIT 8

amendment
asylum

bear arms
believe
capital crime
career counselor
charitable
civic
community health worker
commuters
conserve
eligible
environmental issues
health education specialist
immigrant

impartial
marriage and family
    therapist
naturalization
opinion
peaceably assemble
probation officer /
    correctional treatment
    specialist
protect
punishment
refugee
rehabilitation counselor

resource
reusable
rights
school counselor
slavery
social and human service
    assistant
social welfare
social workers
status
substance abuse,
    behavioral disorder and
    mental health counselor

Stand Out Grammar Reference

UNIT 1

Review: *Be*

Subject	Past	Present	Future
I	was	am	will be
You / We / They	were	are	will be
He / She / It	was	is	will be

Review: Simple Verb Forms

Subject	Past	Present	Future	
He / She / It	studied	studies	will study	English every day.
We	put	put	will put	our studies first.
They	worked	work	will work	too many hours.

Future Perfect

Subject	*will have*	Past Participle		Future Event—Time Expression
I	will have	become	a teacher	**by** the time my kids are in school.
He	will have	been	a graphic designer (for five years)	**when** he turns 35.
They	will have	found	a job	**by** 2017.

We use the future perfect to talk about an activity that will be completed before another time or event in the future. present ✕ future to be completed (perfect) ✕ future event with time expression

Note: The order of events is not important. If the future event with the time expression comes first, use a comma.

Example: *By the time my kids are in school, I will have become a teacher.*

UNIT 2

Past Perfect Continuous					
First Event in Past					**Second Event in Past**
Subject	*had*	*been*	**Verb + *-ing***		
Kimla	had	been	buying	designer clothes	before she started bargain hunting.
He	had	been	buying	coffee at a coffee shop	before he began making it at home.
They	had	been	paying	a lower deductible	before they called the insurance company.
Uses					
<ul><li>We use the past perfect continuous to talk about an activity that was happening for a while before another event happened in the past. For the most recent event, we use the simple past.</li><li>Remember to use a comma if you put the second event as the first part of the sentence. *Before she started bargain hunting, Kimla had been buying designer clothes.*</li></ul>					

UNIT 4

Causative Verbs: *Get, Have, Help, Make, Let*			
Subject	**Verb**	**Noun / Pronoun**	**Infinitive (Omit *to* except with *get*.)**
He	will get	his handyman	to come.
She	had	her mom	wait for the repairperson.
The landlord	helped	me	move in.
Ming Mei	makes	her sister	pay half of the rent.
Mr. Martin	let	Ming Mei	skip one month's rent.
Uses			
We use causative verb structures to indicate that the subject causes something to happen.			

UNIT 5

Adverb Clauses of Concession	
Dependent Clause	**Independent Clause**
Although he spends a lot of time in Las Vegas,	he says he doesn't have a gambling problem.
Even though her sister spends thousands of dollars a month,	she doesn't think she is a shopaholic.
Though she has to drink two cups of coffee before she can get out of bed in the morning,	she is convinced she isn't addicted to caffeine.
In spite of the fact that he plays video games for three hours a night,	he denies he has a problem.

Explanation: Adverb clauses of concession show a contrast in ideas. The main or independent clauses show the unexpected outcome. The unexpected outcome in the third example is that it is surprising that she thinks she isn't addicted to caffeine.

Note: The clauses can be reversed and have the same meaning. Do not use a comma if the independent clause comes first in the sentence.

Example: *She doesn't think she is a shopaholic even though she spends thousands of dollars a month.*

UNIT 6

Appositives		
Noun or Noun Phrase	**Appositive**	**Remainder of Sentence (Predicate)**
The ad,	**the one with all the great pictures,**	makes me want to buy those dishes.
That computer,	**the fastest machine in the store,**	sells for over $2,000.

Explanation:
- An appositive is a noun or noun phrase that renames another noun next to it in a sentence.
- The appositive adds extra descriptive detail, explains, or identifies something about the noun. If the appositive is taken out of the sentence, the sentence still makes sense.
- An appositive can come before or after the noun phrase it is modifying.

Example: *A helpful gift, money is always appreciated by a newly married couple.*

Note: Appositives are usually set off by commas.

UNIT 7

Noun Clauses as Objects		
Subject + Verb	**Noun Clause**	**Explanation**
I did	*what* I was asked.	• A noun clause starts with a question word or *that* and is followed by a subject and verb.
She knows	*how* the computer works.	
They decided	*where* the location would be.	
My boss asked	*who* would be best for the job.	• In these examples, the noun clauses are the objects of the sentences.
I hope	*that* they work as a team.	

UNIT 8

Transitional Expressions		
One reason	The *first* reason	*Some* people
⇓	⇓	⇓
Another reason	The *second* reason	*Other* people
⇓	⇓	⇓
Still another reason	The *third* reason	*Still* others

- Use these phrases to connect your ideas.
- Choose the set of phrases that works best for your topic.
- Don't shift back and forth among sets of phrases.

Text Credits

20 "Educational Attainment and Earning Power for Men and Women 18 and Over" chart. **Source:** Current Population Survey, U.S. Department of Labor, U.S. Bureau of Labor Statistics **Website:** https://www.bls.gov/emp/chart-unemployment-earnings-education.htm; **53** "The Four Keys to Great Credit" **Source:** MSN Money **Website:** money.msn.com; **85** "Seat Belt Use in the States, 2014–2019" **Source:** Seat Belt Use in 2013—Use Rates in the States and Territories, National Highway Traffic Safety Administration **Website:** https://crashstats.nhtsa.dot.gov/Api/Public/ViewPublication/813307; **86** "Facts on alcohol-related accidents" **Source:** Centers for Disease Control and Prevention **Website:** https://www.cdc.gov/transportationsafety/impaired_driving/index.html; **113** "Theft prevention newsletter"

Source: Burglary Prevention, Jefferson County Sherriff's Department, MO **Website:** http://www.jcsd.org/burglary_prevention.htm; **136** "Percentage of persons without health insurance, by age group using three measures of non-coverage, and percentage of persons with health insurance at the time of interview, by coverage type and age group: United States, January–March 2014" **Source:** Health Insurance Coverage: Early Release of Estimates From the National Health Interview Survey, January–March 2014 **Website:** http://www.cdc.gov/nchs/data/nhis/earlyrelease/insur201409.pdf; **137, 138, 149** "Demographic Variation in Health Insurance Coverage: United States, 2020" **Source:** National Center for Health Statistics, National Health

Statistics Report, February 2022 **Website:** https://www.cdc.gov/nchs/data/nhsr/nhsr169.pdf; **195** "Conflict Resolution: Resolving Conflict Rationally and Effectively" **Source:** Mind Tools **Website:** http:// mindtools.com; **215–216** "U.S. Citizenship and Immigration Services" **Source:** USCIS **Website:** http://uscis.gov; **220** "Big Brothers Big Sisters of Eastern Massachusetts **Source:** Big Brothers Big Sisters of Eastern Massachusetts **Website:** https://emassbigs.org/; **223** "Create Less Trash" **Source:** Sustainable Environment for Quality of Life **Website:** http://www.centralina.org; **224** "Carpooling—What is it?" **Source:** Sustainable Environment for Quality of Life **Website:** http://www.centralina.org

Photo Credits

ILLUSTRATIONS: Illustrations created by Oscar Hernandez. All illustrations and graphics are owned by © Cengage Learning, Inc.

PHOTOS: v (tl) © Charlie Zevon, (tr) © Priscilla Caraveo; **xii** (tl) Shapecharge/E+/Getty Images, (tc) (tr) © Christopher Payne/Esto, (cl1) (cr2) © Chris Crisman Photography, (cl2) (cr1) © Brian Doben Photography; **2** (tr) (br) © Chris Crisman Photography, (cl) Shapecharge/E+/Getty Images, (c) (bl) © Brian Doben Photography, (cr) (bc) © Christopher Payne/Esto; **6** (tl) Audtakorn Sutarmjam/Alamy Stock Photo, (tc) Iya Forbes/Moment/Getty Images, (tr) Yasser Chalid/Moment Open/Getty Images; **11** Oscar Wong/Moment/Getty Images; **12–13** (Spread) Jianan Yu/Reuters; **14** (tl) Andrey_Popov/Shutterstock.com, (tr) Westend61/Getty Images, (bl) SeventyFour/Shutterstock.com, (br) FatCamera/E+/Getty Images; **18** Glowimages/Getty Images; **28** (cl) Andrey_Popov/Shutterstock.com, (cr) Juanmonino/E+/Getty Images, (bl1) Westend61/Getty Images, (bl2) FatCamera/E+/Getty Images, (br1) SeventyFour/Shutterstock.com, (br2) Fotoluminate LLC/Shutterstock.com; **39** © Pearl Jennings/National Geographic Image Collection; **40–41** (Spread) Westend61/Getty Images; **56** (tl) Jason cox/Shutterstock.com, (tc) Jose Luis Pelaez Inc/DigitalVision/Getty Images, (tr) Maxuser/Shutterstock.com; **67** © Jannese Torres-Rodriguez/Delish Dlites LLC; **68–69** (Spread) © Matthieu Paley/Paleymotion Ltd; **77** Rudi_suardi/E+/Getty Images; **84** Jojoo64/Shutterstock.com; **95** © Laura Barisonzi; **96–97** (Spread) © Steve Weinik; **108** (tl1) Valery Sidelnykov/Shutterstock.com, (tl2) Ilbusca/E+/Getty Images, (tc1) Banner/Shutterstock.com, (tc2) Stephen Dalton/Minden Pictures/Getty Images, (tr1) Stefan90/iStock/Getty Images, (tr2) JGI/Jamie Grill/Tetra Images/Getty Images; **110** Forestpath/Shutterstock.com; **113** Sdecoret/Shutterstock.com; **114** Michael Vi/Shutterstock.com; **123** Education Images/Universal Images Group/Getty Images; **124** Gorodenkoff/iStock/Getty Images; **126–127** (Spread) RichLegg/Getty Images; **130** (cl) Zeljkosantrac/E+/Getty Images, (c) Lightpoet/Shutterstock.com, (cr) IndianFaces/Shutterstock.com; **140** Andrey_Popov/Shutterstock.com; **153** © The Jane Goodall Institute; **154–155** (Spread) Sean Gallup/Getty Images News/Getty Images; **170** (cl) Artur_Nyk/Shutterstock.com, (bl) Stockphoto-graf/Shutterstock.com; **181** Picture alliance/Getty Images; **182–183** (Spread) Davis Turner/Bloomberg/Getty Images; **184** (tl) Africa Studio/Shutterstock.com, (tc) Photoongraphy/Shutterstock.com, (tr) Chursina Viktoriia/Shutterstock.com, (cl) Peter Dazeley/Photodisc/Getty Images, (c) Sylvie Bouchard/Shutterstock.com, (cr) Apveanz/Shutterstock.com, (bl) Taras Vyshnya/Alamy Stock Photo, (bc) Roman Samokhin/Shutterstock.com, (br) i viewfinder/Shutterstock.com; **186** (tr) Proxima Studio/Shutterstock.com, (c) Fizkes/Shutterstock.com, (cr1) Andrey_Popov/Shutterstock.com, (cr2) Imagebroker/Alamy Stock Photo, (bc) Kpatyhka/Shutterstock.com, (br) Daniel Krason/Shutterstock.com; **209** Alistair Berg/DigitalVision/Getty Images; **210–211** (Spread) New York On Air/Offset/Shutterstock.com; **214** (cl1) DragonImages/iStock/Getty Images, (cl2) Jetta Productions/Blend Images/Getty Images, (bl1) StockLite/Shutterstock.com, (bl2) Monkey Business Images/Shutterstock.com, (bl3) Daniel Ernst/iStock/Getty Images; **221** (tl) Seyomedo/Shutterstock.com, (tr) Mojca Odar/Shutterstock.com, (cl) MGP/DigitalVision/Getty Images, (cr) Esa Hiltula/Alamy Stock Photo; **225** (tl) Vadim Petrakov/Shutterstock.com, (tc) Chaoss/Shutterstock.com, (tr) AVN Photo Lab/Shutterstock.com; **237** Bettmann/Getty Images; **238** (tr1) Radu Bercan/Shutterstock.com, (tr2) L F File/Shutterstock.com.

Stand Out Skills Index

ACADEMIC SKILLS

Brainstorming, 33, 59, 71, 73, 93, 102, 113, 139, 146, 179, 201, 207, 208, 226, 228, 236

Calculations
Gas mileage and cost per mile, 82

Categorizing, Classifying 7, 87, 98, 128, 157, 192, 213

Charts, graphs, and diagrams, 3, 7, 16, 19, 20, 29, 32, 33, 38, 46, 59–61, 71–73, 81–83, 87, 89, 90, 98, 100, 113, 114, 116, 122, 128, 136, 137, 146, 149, 152, 157, 162, 169, 174, 185, 190, 201, 207, 213, 228, 229, 231, 236

Critical thinking
Advise, 54, 131
Analyze, 45, 48, 82, 107, 137, 140, 146, 198, 216, 219, 228
Apply, 5, 21, 144
Brainstorm, 33, 59, 71, 73, 93, 102, 113, 139, 146, 179, 201, 207, 208, 226, 228, 236
Calculate, 44, 45, 82, 83, 90, 110
Categorize, 87, 98, 128, 157, 192, 213
Classify, 87, 98, 128, 157, 192, 213
Collaborate, 37, 65, 93, 179
Compare, 3, 22, 29, 50, 114, 117, 122
Compose, 8, 11, 24, 228
Contrast, 109
Create, 4, 114, 132, 138, 166, 172, 222
Decide, 30, 49, 86
Define, 15, 16, 19, 28, 31, 50, 75, 83, 87, 92, 99, 106, 112, 120, 139, 143, 180, 185, 212, 234, 236
Evaluate, 16, 18, 24, 79, 130, 160, 163, 215, 223
Explain, 184
Infer, 6, 9, 15, 42, 43, 94, 129, 212
Imagine, 73
Interpret, 104, 174, 219
Justify, 46
Plan, 111
Predict, 38, 50, 66, 94, 113, 152, 195, 208, 214

Prioritize, 27
Research, 73, 160
Restate, 106, 165
Role-play, 147, 169, 190
Solve, 191, 228
Summarize, 33, 52, 58, 77, 104, 105, 152, 186, 208, 217
Visualize, 141

Drawing, 185, 192

Editing, 10, 24, 165

Grammar
Adverb clauses of concession, 141
Appositives, 171
Be, 22
Causative verbs, 101
Future perfect, 30
Noun clauses as objects, 199
Parts of speech, 194
Past perfect continuous, 49
Simple verb forms, 23
Transitional expressions, 228
Word families, 185

Group activities, 7, 8, 10, 18, 20, 25, 28, 50, 53, 56, 58, 66, 72, 73, 83, 84, 86, 93, 94, 104, 107, 113, 117, 121, 130, 136, 138, 140, 149, 151, 152, 158, 163, 179, 189, 207, 208, 216, 219, 220, 226

Learning styles, 16–18

Listening
Conversations, 3–6, 21, 48, 59, 81, 100, 109, 133, 134, 147, 158, 162, 167, 169, 190
Descriptions, 22, 130
Interviews, 57
Introductions, 5
Lectures, 16, 26, 216
Questions, 160
Statistics, 112
Tips, 82, 83, 114

Matching, 18, 38, 79, 92, 94, 99, 101, 109, 115, 139, 178, 187, 190, 205, 218

Multiple-choice questions, 26, 57, 60, 66, 80, 122, 140, 150, 166, 168, 177, 196, 204

Partner activities, 4, 6, 8, 19, 21, 22–24, 27–29, 33, 35, 36, 42, 44, 46, 47, 51, 54, 55, 59, 63, 71, 74–76, 78, 79, 83–87, 90, 92

Prioritizing, 27

Reading
Ads, 47, 117, 170, 203
Advice, 131
Articles, 39, 50, 53–54, 67, 76, 77, 95, 103, 123, 132, 153, 181, 188, 195, 197, 209, 224, 237
Bill of Rights, 217, 219
Careers, 33, 145, 147, 175
Charts and graphs, 85, 110, 111, 138, 174, 189, 201, 202, 229
Conversations, 3–5, 81, 100, 134, 167
Descriptions, 220–222
Email messages, 9, 11
First aid procedures, 144
Flyers, 25
Instructions, 186,
Insurance policies, 78, 80, 91, 119, 138
Introductions, 3–5, 204
Lists, 29, 42, 48
Main ideas, 50–51
Maintenance and repair guides, 76, 77
Newsletter, 113
Paragraphs, 23, 227
Price policies, 168
Product reviews, 159
Rental agreements, 103–105
Report guidelines, 198
Reports, 198
Return policies, 177
Sentences, 43, 102, 212, 218
Spreadsheets, 45, 62
Statistics, 86
Texts, 100
Thank-you notes, 10
Troubleshooting tips, 204
Warranties and guarantees, 164–166
Websites, 215

Research strategies, 37, 65, 207

Speaking
Answering questions, 21, 23, 136
Asking questions, 8, 21, 24, 33
Conversations, 138

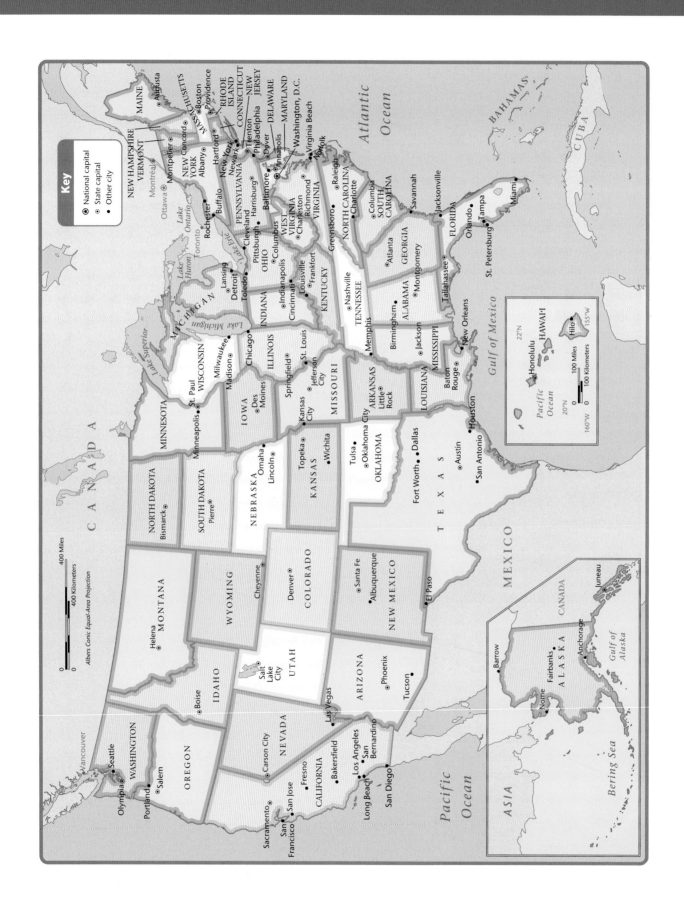